THE GLITTERING ILLUSION

THE LAND OF VIRGINIA

The Virgin Queen, King's River, Old Dominion:
    This is the land that England found.
Northumberland south to Sussex, now Virginian
    —But tobacco stirred in English ground.

The nightingale became a whippoorwill,
    Though English Church upheld the throne;
A softer speech spread westward, courteous still,
    And cornbread overcame the scone.

The sea-wave hills of Piedmont signalling
    Blue mountains thrust against the light—
That flash of blue on country roads in spring
    Through Judas-tree rose and dogwood white.

The vision of Home beyond the seas grew pale,
    The land found legends of her own:
The knights who rode with Spotswood told a tale;
    Then tales of Redcoats overthrown.

And greater than all, the thunder of Stuart's horse,
    Bright cavalier; and Stonewall's tread;
The courteous strength of Lee: undying source
    Of lost-cause legends of the mythic dead.

The question haunts us still: Why God would let
    Such men—and freedom—fail to stand?
Down fleeting years, we never quite forget
    The tragic grandeur in our land.

Sheldon Vanauken

THE GLITTERING ILLUSION

English Sympathy
for the
Southern Confederacy

by Sheldon Vanauken

Regnery Gateway
Washington, D.C.

Library of Congress Cataloging-in-Publication Data

Vanauken, Sheldon.
  The glittering illusion : English sympathy for the Southern
Confederacy / by Sheldon Vanauken : with a foreword by Lord Beloff.
    p.   cm.
  Includes bibliographical references.
  ISBN 0-89526-552-4
  1. United States—History—Civil War, 1861–1865—Foreign public
opinion, British. 2. United States—Foreign relations—1861–1865.
3. Confederate States of America—Foreign public opinion, British.
4. Public opinion—Great Britain—History—19th century. I. Title.
E469.8.V36   1989
973.7—dc20   89-36927
                                                                  CIP

Published in the United States by
Regnery Gateway
1130 17th Street, NW
Washington, DC 20036

Distributed to the trade by
National Book Network
4720-A Boston Way
Lanham, MD 20706

This book is set in English Times typestyle.

Previously published in the United Kingdom by Churchman Publishing Ltd., 1988.

Manufactured in the United States of America.

10 9 8 7 6 5 4 3 2 1

House of Lords

Mr Sheldon Vanauken has shown a singular consistency
in pursuing an idea that was originally the subject
of his graduate research at Oxford University to
its presentation in this volume. Mr Vanauken believes
- and there is a good deal of evidence to support
him - that English sympathies during the American
Civil War were largely on the southern side of
the conflict. British intervention would have secured
a southern victory which might have suited British
commercial interests and British conceptions of
the balance of power and put an end to American
hopes of annexing Canada. Support for the South
would have conformed to the general British disposition
to give credence to struggles for national self-
determination. Why then, did Britain not intervene
as at one moment she seemed on the point of doing?
Mr Sheldon Vanauken dismisses the view that British
anti-slavery sentiment and hence popular support
for the northern cause was the root of the matter
and plumps for what he calls the "Glittering Illusion"
namely the belief that southern military skills,
and in particular the generalship of Robert E. Lee,
were thought to make a southern defeat unthinkable,
so that the South could win its independence without
the foreign assistance that the American colonies
had enjoyed in winning their independence from the
British Empire in the war of the American Revolution.
It is an interesting idea and one that challenges
many accepted beliefs. Interesting also are Mr
Vanauken's subsequent speculations on what would
have happened if the South had actually won and
as he believes would have followed had freed its
slaves of its own volition. A truly unusual book
by a Virginian anglophile.

Beloff

Formerly Gladstone Professor of Government and
Public Administration in the University of Oxford

This book is dedicated to my wife
Davy/Jean who by making it her own every
step of the way made it better—
and made it fun.

Author's Note

This book on English sympathy and even love for the van-
ished nation represented by Lee and Jackson and Stuart was
originally written in Oxford, well known to be (in Matthew Arnold's words) the "home of lost causes, and forsaken beliefs,
and unpopular names, and impossible loyalties." The research
was chiefly done in the Bodleian Library, especially in its vast
and apparently untouched collection of contemporary pamphlets.
Although the author had previously worked in Southern history
(e.g., "A Century of the Southern Plantation" in *The Virginia
Magazine of History and Biography,* July 1950), *The Glittering
Illusion* is a work in English history, an almost forgotten chapter.
It was first written in 1952, revised in 1957, and further revised
in preparation for the present publication. The two special essays
in the Epilogue were published in *The Southern Partisan*
magazine in Spring and Summer of 1984 and are used by
permission.

Contents

Reference Notes are at end of chapters.

Prologue

The Question

The four-year war between the American states came to an end in 1865 with the overwhelming defeat of the Southern states and the disappearance of their government, the Confederate States of America. Only five years after the end of the war, an English historian was writing that English sympathy for the Southern Confederacy "in truth...was so far from being dominant that any English Government which should have determined to interfere could not have retained office for a month, and any Minister who was known to have proposed it would have irretrievably ruined his own political career."[1] A post-war English traveller in the United States informed his hosts that during the war English newspapers "did not reflect the real sentiments of the nation".[2] W.E.H. Lecky wrote at the end of the century that "throughout the war a majority of the population remained, I believe, steadily on the side of the North."[3] Justin McCarthy wrote, more cautiously: "It is not certain that the supporters of the Southern side at any time actually outnumbered the champions of the North and of the Union".[4] In the twentieth century, E.D. Adams wrote of the "tide of democratic feeling...rising in England" and of the "whole-hearted support of Radical England" for the North.[5] Jordan and Pratt wrote: "Although not actually very numerous, these 'Southerners' seemed stronger than they were".[6]

But in the course of the war, between 1861 and 1865, James Mason, Confederate States Commissioner to England, wrote confidentially to his Secretary of State in Richmond, Virginia, that "there can be no mistake that with all classes in England which have an opinion, their entire sympathy is with us."[7] Captain James Bulloch, C.S.N., wrote that "personal observation, confirmed by the testimony of every other agent of the Confederate Government whose duties compelled him to reside in England..., convinced me that the great majority of the people in Great Britain—at least among the classes a traveller, or a man of business, or a frequenter of the clubs, would be likely to meet—were on the Southern side."[8] Lest this be supposed but Southern optimism, the United States Consul at Liverpool wrote: "It was very evident from the commencement that the South...had the sympathy of the people of England...I speak now of the great mass of the English people."[9] Henry Adams, the son and secretary of the United States Minister in London, wrote: "As for this country, the simple fact is that it is unanimously against us and becomes more firmly set every day."[10] An English partisan of the North wrote to a member of the opposite camp about the Southern supporters: "I fear you do not overstate your constituency when you put it at three-fourths of educated Englishmen".[11] After a debate in the House of Commons on recognition of the Confederacy, *The Manchester Guardian* said that the debate "should not be thought to have anything to do with the sentiments and sympathies of the English people, for these were entirely with the South".[12] The Manager of *The Times* wrote to a strongly pro-Southern correspondent: "Your views are entirely in accordance with those of the paper & I believe of the majority in this country".[13] The pro-Northern *Spectator* said: "The educated million in England, with here and there an exception, have become unmistakably Southern."[14]

There is a difference between the wartime accounts and the postwar ones; there is a decided difference. How is it to be explained? There is, of course, a natural wish to be on the winning side. Men tend to keep quiet about the causes they favoured when those causes are defeated. Biographers, desiring to display their subjects in the most favourable light, may say little of the times when they were wrong. Matthew Arnold, speaking of the middle classes and the war, said that "they were 'full of coldness, slights, and sermons' for the Federals, and, as soon as the Federals were victorious, discovered that they had always wished them well.'"[15] How much of the difference between the contemporary and the subsequent accounts of the sympathy for the South can be attributed to the simple fact that the North won the war? Had the Confederate States secured their independence, should we read in the histories that England had always been Southern?

It is my purpose to attempt an answer to these questions. There are difficulties in that, after the event, men *were* quiet, shrouding their partisanship of the Southern cause in silence, or having that service performed for them by their biographers, while for the nation the same service was performed by historians. For I cannot escape the impression that there has been a persistent minimizing of the sympathy for the South, a tendency to accept uncritically such contemporary accounts as suggest sympathy for the North and to discount or ignore those which give a different impression. I have come to believe that English sympathy for the South can only be compared, in intensity and identification with its object, to English sympathy for Greece and Italy in their struggles for freedom; and yet in the general histories it is, if mentioned at all, scarcely so portrayed. If I am right about the passion and enthusiasm of this sympathy, its comparative neglect can only be attributed to the fact that it led to nothing: the North won; more important, *democracy* won.

This is a study of English sympathy for the Southern Confederary. There is little that can be added on the subject of English sympathy for the Union, since all—if not more than all—the evidence has been presented. Northern sympathy will be touched on here in connexion with the limits of the Southern. But primarily we are concerned with the English friends of the South. Too often it has been suggested by historians that, while Northern sympathy was sincere, disinterested, idealistic, and somewhat greater than the evidence

would lead one to believe, Southern sympathy was confined to a
few, selfish and insincere, wealthy men. I disagree. I believe that
there were ideals as well as practical considerations on both sides,
but that generous enthusiasm was more often to be found among
the friends of the South. Since this is a study of opinion in England
in the years of and in relation to the war between the American
states, it is necessarily limited to those who had an opinion on the
matter, but nearly every literate Englishman did have. England was
intensely aware of the war and of at least some of the issues involved. Precisely what is meant by 'England', and by public opinion,
will be explored in later pages. Here it is enough to say that this
is a study of English opinion principally in relation to England's
sympathy with the Southern Confederacy: the origins of that sympathy, its nature and bases, its extent and force. And one thing
more—why it failed, if it was so great, to move England to some
sort of action intended to ensure the independence of the South.

Perhaps one cautionary note is advisable: The South—and the
North—here portrayed is that which Englishmen saw; it is not
necessarily the South as it saw itself, although it is not so far from
that, nor is it the South as American historians variously see it today. The embattled South that England saw was aristocratic and
thoroughly English—a land of chivalrous gentlemen—and it was
made up principally of Virginia and Carolina. If there were some
rough democratic types in the hills or some states with difficult
names like Tennessee or Mississippi, they were largely ignored. The
North was, if anything, more distorted in English eyes. Moreover,
however clear their sight, they were quite unable to see the changes
a passing century has wrought: Abraham Lincoln wore no halo for
them and they did not perceive—indeed, could not have believed—
the huge and firmly reunited America that was to be.

The Confederacy staked all on what was considered, not only
by Southerners but by many Englishmen, the virtual certainty of
English intervention. And yet England, the world's greatest con-
sumer of raw cotton, did not in four long years of war do what

it had been thought one year of cotton hunger would force her to do. In the break-up of the 'Model Republic' across the Atlantic, English aristocrats saw the final discrediting of democracy—at the hands, they were pleased to discover, of a fellow Anglo-Saxon aristocracy. But they could not have failed to realize that they themselves would suffer a serious, perhaps mortal, blow if the South went down. England's continued neutrality, not Gettysburg, was the chief lost battle of the Confederacy. And it was a major lost battle of aristocracy everywhere.

Yet in the war years the sympathy for the South was a strongly running tide that skilled observers expected would sweep England into the war. A contemporary writer likened the sympathy for the South to a torrent and that for the North to a dam; he thought, more than once, that the dam was about to go. Was the flood, in fact, less than he thought? or was the dam stronger?

The answer, I believe, was neither of these. We shall examine the springs of the sympathy for the Confederacy, and then its full flood; and we shall see that it was great enough to sweep away the dam. And, lastly, we shall examine the fundamental misconception—the glittering illusion—that operated as a spillway or floodgate to draw off all excess pressure on the dam.

[1] M. Bernard, *A Historical Account of the Neutrality of Great Britain During the American Civil War*, London, 1870, p 467.

[2] W.E. Adams, *Our American Cousins*, London, 1883, p 351.

[3] W.E.H. Lecky, *Democracy & Liberty*, 2 vol., London, 1899, v I, p 485. [Hereafter: Lecky]

[4] J. McCarthy, *A History of Our Own Times*, 4 vol., London, 1880, v III, p 335. [Hereafter: McCarthy]

[5] E.D. Adams, *Great Britain & the American Civil War*, 2 vol., London, 1925, v II, pp 291 & 305. [Hereafter: E.D. Adams]

[6] D. Jordan & E.J. Pratt, *Europe & the American Civil War*, Boston, 1931, pp 162-163. [Hereafter: Jordan & Pratt]

[7] Virginia Mason, *The Public Life & Diplomatic Correspondence of James M. Mason*, New York, 1906, p 465. [Hereafter: Mason]

[8] J.D. Bulloch, *The Secret Service of the Confederate States in Europe*, 2 vol., London, 1883, v II, p 303. [Hereafter: Bulloch]

[9] T.H. Dudley, *Three Critical Periods in our Diplomatic Relations with England During the Late War*, Reprint from *The Pennsylvania Magazine of History & Biography*, April, 1893, p 3.

[10] W.C. Ford, Ed., *A Cycle of Adams Letters 1861-1865*, 2 vol., Boston & New York, 1920, v I, p 140.

[11] Mrs. A.P. Bayman, *Notes & Letters on the American War by an English "Lady"*, London, 1864, p 56.

[12] Quoted by Jordan & Pratt, p 109.

[13] *The History of the Times: The Tradition Established 1841-1884* (vol. II), London, 1939, p 389. [Hereafter: *The Times* (History)]

[14] Quoted by J.F. Rhodes, *History of the United States from the Compromise of 1850 to the McKinley-Bryan Campaign of 1896*, 8 vol., New York, 1920, v IV, p 340. [Hereafter: Rhodes]

[15] Quoted by O.F. Christie, *The Transition from Aristocracy 1832-1867*, London, 1927, p 225.

Part I Springs

Chapter One

The England of 1860

Chapter Two

The Events of 1861

Chapter One

The England of 1860

The impact of the American War of Secession upon England caused a reaction subtly, and in some respects radically, different to such a war in 1830 or 1890. We are here concerned with the England, the English people, of 1860, and we must try to see in broad outline their positon with regard to the affairs at home and abroad that are relevant to the attitudes they later assumed towards the contenders in America. There cannot be, within the scope of this work, a thorough portrait. Indeed, a 'living likeness' is well-nigh impossible, for, although these Englishmen used most of the words we shall use—democracy, war, slavery, reform, the Colonies, the United States, France—in much the same sort of context, the overtones and perhaps the very meanings were uncapturably different to our own or even to those of 1830 and 1890. To give this truism significant life, we need only to contemplate the ring of the phrase 'the next war' as *we* hear it under the shadow of the Bomb, and as *they* heard it in 1860 when the Crimean War—that affair of blundering professionals and one intrepid woman—was in the recent past. This sure difference, though, makes it the more essential to attempt at least the salient features of the English people in the period of Lord Palmerston's last Ministry.

With Regard to Affairs at Home

In the year before 1860, after winning a General Election with
a small majority, Palmerston with Lord John Russell and
Gladstone—the 'Triumvirate'—had formed a coalition Government,
which endured through the American war until the death of
Palmerston in 1865. It was, perhaps, the last Whig Government,
or the last of that Whig-Liberalism which first came into power as
a result of the First Reform Bill; it might almost be called also the
first Liberal Government with its middle-class free-trader members.
Each of the three leaders at times favoured recognition of the independence of the Confederate States of America. Gladstone and
Palmerston, at least, sympathized with the South. With vigorous
agreement the 'Triumvirate' could probably have carried the Cabinet
and undoubtedly both Houses of Parliament; and yet this powerful Ministry played an indecisive and negative part in the years of
the war.

But in 1860 the question had not arisen. The great issue was
reform, a subdued issue that was yet underlying everything: reform
not today but tomorrow or the day after. The first Reform Bill,
which had been intended to fortify the nation against revolution
by extending the franchise to the middle class, was nearly a third
of a century in the past. The reforming drive of the Whigs was spent;
home affairs for nearly a decade had ceased to be of first importance. Franchise bills were introduced—there were several of them
in the fifties—but they came to nothing and were quickly forgotten. Palmerston took office in tacit agreement with the Tories that
reform was to be shelved, while Russell, although not quite so certain as he had been, had acquired the nickname of 'Finality Jack'
from his statement that the Reform Bill of 1832 was final. Many
believed, and said with varying degrees of vigour, that England could
not safely proceed further with reform. Nevertheless, there remained
the unspoken, and perhaps in some cases unadmitted, awareness
that sooner or later England must face up to the question of extend-

ing the franchise.

Power in the realm of England had, by the enfranchisement of 1832, passed to the middle class, but the reins of power continued to be held by the upper class; even as after 1867, when real power began to descend to the lower class, the middle class governed. Both Palmerston and Russell represented the old Whigs, as conservative in most respects as the Tories themselves. There was, in fact, very little difference between the parties in 1860: most of the legislation, regardless of party, was inspired by Liberalism, and most of the leaders were aristocrats. Sometimes one finds it difficult to remember, when reading of the vigorous and dominant aristocracy, that the world of Queen Victoria was in reality basically commercial and middle-class. But the able, intelligent aristocrats not only carried themselves with an ancient authority but took the lead in good works and other matters dear to the middle-class heart. England, as Gladstone said, had "a sneaking kindness for a lord".

Nevertheless, despite the country's traditional government and unequalled prosperity, there were, under the serene surface of the year 1860, forces of change abroad in the land. Liberalism, checked only by the survival of Palmerston, stood ready, in the earnest and representative person of Gladstone, to transform the Whig Party. For its ideas and much of its force Liberalism drew upon its Radical Wing—sometimes called the Manchester School—whose ideas were ably expounded by John Bright and Richard Cobden. Their simple doctrine was made up of free trade and free competition and progress—all unlimited. They hated war, distrusted aristocracy, and saw no use in the Empire. They were at once practical business men and sincere Christians: a harmony, not an opposition, in their view. In fact, it might be said that the Liberalism of 1860 rested upon two bases, Jeremy Bentham's Utilitarianism and Evangelical Christianity. And both were pervaded by nineteenth-century humanitarianism, which is not clearly traceable to either, and by the over-extended evolutionary concepts that were 'in the air'. Since the latter were being clarified and stressed by the *Origin of the*

Species, published a year earlier, they may be called 'Darwinism'; from them came the idea of infinite progress towards greater and greater prosperity and towards an end to wars. Darwinian also was the justification for unlimited competition: the survival of the fit.

Utilitarianism, with its stress on pleasure as the goal of life, might be thought opposed to Christian aims. So it is; but the operative idea of mid-century Utilitarianism was the familiar criterion, the greatest good of the greatest number, which is not necessarily opposed to Christianity. There was no opposition between them, for instance, when it came to freeing the slaves (although there might have been). Moreover, Benthamism stood for business efficiency and admired the competent self-supporting business man. Thus war could be, and was, simultaneously condemned as wasteful and inefficient, as not for the greatest good of the greatest number, and as contrary to Christian principles. Similarly, it was a mixture of Evangelical and Utilitarian concepts that led middle-class business men like Cobden and Bright, following the star of progress, to champion the cause of the working man—with such success that he succeeded to their power.

This unselfishness and a sort of winning sincerity about these men and their fellows were the results of their Christianity. Evangelicalism—in the Church of England and among the Nonconformists alike—is a peculiarly English phenomenon, owing much to the Wesleys and more to the English character. Since, today, we are not always inclined to see the business man as God's ally, we shall find it rewarding to examine a little more closely this force that had done so much to improve the conditions in prisons, to destroy the slave trade, and to instill the idea of respectability. The roots of Evangelicalism were Puritan; although it lacked the stern excesses of Scotch Calvinism, it had something of the same narrowness of outlook. Early Evangelicals were intensely aware of their own sinful state and God's just wrath as well as their hope of salvation through Christ. But the strength of Evangelicalism did not lie in theology or scholarship, where it was in truth rather feeble, but

in the application of their truths to everyday life. It was a creed
of action and, while the enthusiasm was still in them, the
Evangelicals were intent on attacking and correcting the evils they
could see. They fought against child labour and vice at home and
slavery in the Empire and reduced them. They supported
'temperance' and discredited duelling. England became less gay and
careless, more sober and responsible; Sunday was observed, and
sermons were read as well as heard. Few cared or dared to defy
this power of earnest morality. But the emphasis on Respectability, present from the first in this essentially middle-class movement,
survived the fervour of the first decades to become dominant:
England became a respectable, a *proper* nation in look and word
and, perhaps, thought. Gaiety and wit seemed vaguely suspect. And,
as the genuine religious enthusiasm waned, men discovered that "the
virtues of a Christian after the Evangelical model were easily ex-
changeable with the virtues of a successful merchant or a rising
manufacturer, and that a more than casual analogy could be
established between Grace and Corruption and the Respectable and
the Low."[1] As monarchs and aristocrats before them and, more
weakly, socialists after them, the merchants drew upon the words
of the courteous Christ to keep the established stars in the local sky.

   So in 1860 England presented herself to the world as a devoutly
religious nation, rightly rewarded for her virtue by wealth and power.
The churches were full and new churches—in a doubtful Gothic—
were being built. And, in truth, there was much sincere faith. The
Anglo-Catholic Revival set in motion by the Oxford Movement was
quietly at work, holding to a grander ideal of the Church, strengthen-
ing the Church by scholarship and a disciplined priesthood. But
the high-church conception of the Church's sphere as limited to
religion limits also our historical interest. Rationalism, it is true,
was also developing, but the deep-rooted humanitarianism of the
period could survive a loss of faith. And Evangelicalism, though
the crusading spirit was on the ebb, was still a force to be reckoned
with. Its chief weakness resulted from its own past success. The

decade before 1860 had been notably free of religious controversies or causes, and Respectability was triumphant. It was respectable to go to church and to be opposed to slavery and vice; everyone, therefore, went to church and was opposed to slavery and vice—but it was to a devitalizing degree a passive compliance. Evangelical Christianity, while still taking itself seriously, tended to grow fat and rather complacent.

The England of 1860 is indeed, on the whole, a comfortably plump and complacent England. There was much sentimentality and lack of taste, but the complacency was rooted in real and immense achievement. But, despite the pleased acceptance of English superiority and things as they were, the forces of change were at work beneath the tranquil surface. Progressive Darwinian England might have indeed expected this, but it could not quite have believed by what devious routes—wars and poverty—the realm was to move towards its chief poet's vision of "the Parliament of Man, the Federation of the World."[2] For England was becoming ever more wealthy, supremely the workshop of the world, and the threats to that supremacy were hardly perceived. Although the landed interests were still powerful, the great industrial and shipping towns grew ever more important. There the trade-unionists were trying their strength and laying the foundations of the effective unions of the future. And there, too, the new ideas of democracy had put down tentative roots. Karl Marx was writing in the England of 1860; and the (Roman) Catholic hierarchy had recently been revived. Not only had the *Origin of the Species* just been published but, in the same year, Edward Fitzgerald's *Omar Khayyam* and J.S. Mill's *Essay on Liberty*.

The last of these, a significant and widely-read book by a chief thinker of the age, dealt—as is commonly the case with essays on liberty—with a tyrant. But the tyrant was neither king nor baron (nor capitalist). People in 1860 were reading a plea for liberty of thought from the tyranny of public opinion. This was not indeed the first voice that had been raised in warning against such a tyrant;

de Tocqueville had likened the tyranny of the majority to the tyranny of an absolute monarch; but this was an English voice warning of an English danger. And it was a danger that was new in the world. Opinion in the eighteenth century could only have meant upper-class opinion, chiefly because there was no power elsewhere to enforce or even to present contrary views. The only significant popular opinion was the dangerous murmur that precedes revolution or uprising. But with the enfranchisement of the middle class and their growing awareness of their power, government found it necessary to give increasing weight to their ideas. The rise of public opinion as a factor in government paralled the decline of the power of the monarchy; in 1860 the self-awareness of the middle class was at its height, and a year later monarchy, in the person of Queen Victoria (upon the death of the Prince Consort), ceased to play an active part in public affairs. But public opinion was not yet the opinion of all the people of England: it was the opinion of the comfortable 'educated million'. Louis Blanc in his intelligent and perceptive *Letters on England* wrote in 1863: "But we should not forget that in this country opinion rules. In speaking of England, the word means, not this or that man, but England simply. . . . The working-classes [however]. . . are not represented in the play of the public powers. Barely are they represented in the press. It is not their opinion, therefore, especially on points of foreign policy, which constitutes OPINION. 'Opinion' on international questions is that which is held by what are here called 'the governing classes.' This it is which provides nations friendly, hostile, or rival to England with the measure of her tendencies and her passions; it is of that foreigners speak when they say 'England.' "3★ In ensuing pages there will be many references to English opinion and to 'England', and the reader should bear in mind that the opinion represents a real factor in life and government yet does not mean, as it would today, the opinion

★ The *Letters on England* (four volumes of them, translated from the French) were written by M. Blanc for papers in France. They will be quoted often in these pages as being particularly valuable in their detached account of English sentiments.

of a majority of all Englishmen; then the opinion that was 'England' was that of the enfranchised, literate, respectable middle, and the upper, classes—the 'educated million'.*

With Regard to the Empire

Three events, none so much as a century distant, shaped the thinking of the Englishman of 1860 with regard to his Empire. The earliest was the breakup of what has been called the First British Empire upon the independence of the Thirteen Colonies. Next was the abolition of slavery in the Empire; and, finally, the complete victory of the principle of free trade.

There were always Englishmen who saw in the revolting colonists simply Englishmen fighting for English rights. Aware of justice in this view, the historically-inclined were also aware that the Colonies had, in fact, had a considerable measure of self-government and that their Rights had not been trampled to the extent that the United States were afterwards fond of asserting. Still, the Colonies *had* revolted, after nearly two centuries of attachment. Therefore, in due course, other colonies would demand independence; and, when they did, it must be granted—without war. This was the teaching of History. She was supported, as is often the case, by the intellectual 'climate' of the time: in this instance by the Darwinian ideas of progress and development. Thus the civil-service head of the Colonial Office in 1860 could write: "I have always believed that the destiny of our colonies is independence; and that in this point of view the function of the Colonial Office is to ensure that our connexion, while it lasts, shall be as profitable to both parties, and our separation, when it comes, as amicable as possible."[4] This same

★ Once the phrase 'England intends' would have meant 'the King intends'; later it might have meant 'the great peers intend'. Now in 1860 (and in this book) it must be taken to mean 'the educated million, or a majority of them, intend'. No doubt many of the lower classes shaped their views on those of their 'betters', but they had little to do with 'England intends'. Many more years must pass before the phrase will mean 'the English people intend'.

sense of inevitability is reflected even earlier by the Radical M.P., John Arthur Roebuck: "No one disputes at this time the assertion, that our provinces in North America must soon be independent." And, more sadly: "They will leave us probably after a rebellion and a war—they will throw themselves upon the United States for assistance."⁵ Thus the Revolution of the Thirteen Colonies to Englishmen suggested—and native uprisings, the Indian Mutiny, and the progress of Canada and Australia towards virtual self-government confirmed—that the normal evolution of colonies was in the direction of independence. England could but bow, gracefully if possible, to the inevitable.

Almost coincidentally with this prototype of modern colonial separations, the then-young-and-ardent Evangelical Movement discovered in the evils of the slave trade an issue that was not obscured, like that in the evils of industrial slavery, by menacing hints of rebellion. The Evangelicals, therefore, fought with single-minded purpose until, having achieved the destruction of the slave trade in 1807, they succeeded a quarter-century later in abolishing slavery itself throughout the Empire. The ending of the slave trade, so far as it was ended, had only a happy effect upon world morality and upon the future of Africa. But the abolition of slavery struck a well-nigh mortal blow at the prosperity of the West Indies; and these glamorous isles, once regarded as the most valuable of British possessions, lost both their glamour and their value. The Negroes refused to assume, as their liberators had hoped, the full stature and dignity of free men; they also—or so the reports seemed to indicate—refused to work and lived a hand-to-mouth existence. The plantation life lost its charm and its profits. While it would be false to suggest that England regretted emancipation, the decline of the Islands contributed to a disillusionment both with regard to the value of empire and with regard to the beneficial effects of freeing the Negro. The latter was expressed near 1860 by Anthony Trollope in a protest against the sentimentality that idealized the freed West Indian: "Certainly, my philanthropic friend, let us regard him well.

He *is* a man, and, if you will, a brother; but he is the very idlest brother with which a hardworking workman was ever cursed, intent only on getting his mess of pottage without giving anything in return."[6] And *The Times,* which had always supported both the abolition of the slave trade and of slavery, said: "There is no blinking the truth.... The freed West India slave will not till the soil for wages... And what matters it to him that the Englishman has sunk his thousands and tens of thousands on mills, machinery, and plants, which now totter on the languishing estate that for years has only returned beggary and debt?...We wish to Heaven that some...honest-hearted, and clear-sighted man—would go out to some of the islands... [and] would watch the precious *protégé* of English philanthropy... as he lazily plants his little squatting... as he proudly rejects agricultural or domestic service... and then come home and teach that memorable lesson of their experience to the fanatics who have perverted him into what he is."[7] England was still opposed to slavery—those who lacked sincere conviction opposing it none the less because to do so was respectable—but there can be little doubt that there had been a decline in the vigour and passion of the abolitionist sentiment. The battle, of course, was won in the British Empire. All were in favour of emancipation everywhere else—no one would dare to advocate slavery—but few were very interested: the fire had sunk and the crusade was over. Only, there was no restoring of the West Indies to a valuable colony.

The third element of the thinking on Empire was free trade. The Mercantile System—the eighteenth-century policy of protecting home industry and maintaining a favourable balance of trade—had caused colonies to be regarded with a cold and business-like eye as producers of raw materials and as markets. This concept of the colonial function in relation to home prosperity, which had a bearing on the loss of the Thirteen, was already declining, partly owing to that loss, by the end of the eighteenth century. The Liberal ideal of free trade took its place and, fought for enthusiastically by the Manchester School, won complete acceptance in 1846 with the fall of the last bastion of protection, the Corn Laws. The landlords wept; the *coup de grâce* was administered to the West Indian planters now exposed to the competition of slave-holding countries; but no one was permitted to stand in the way of the greatest good of the greatest number. Whether the Repeal of the Corn Laws was the reason or not, the 'hungry forties' promptly came to an end; the mid-century prosperity set in; and the Free Traders were confirmed. By 1860, in which year Cobden persuaded Napoleon III to agree to a commercial pact on free-trade principles, free trade had become almost a religion. Such nations as the United States that clung to the outworn idea of protection were looked upon, with pity and irritation, as unenlightened. More important, colonies were no longer valued by those who had seen the 'light', for, since unlimited free trade was sure to create prosperity, there could be no need of protected markets. Indeed, an independent—hence, proud and contented—Canada or Australia would be a better customer, and England would be free of the costly burden of responsibility entailed by empire.

The three strands—inevitable independence of colonies, the decline in value of the plantations from the somewhat disillusioning emancipation, and free trade—twist inseparably together to bridle the empire-builder in the name of 'Little England'. The revolt of the Thirteen and the Darwinian doctrine of development combined to convince England that sooner or later all colonies must have independence. The decline of the West Indies under the twin blows of emancipation and free trade brought home the conviction that a colonial empire was an economic liability belonging to a past order. Evangelical England, vaguely conscious of a slight chill at the results of emancipation and of twenty years' missionary efforts, was not in 1860 quite ready to shoulder what was to be called 'the white man's burden'. The old idea of Empire was practically dead; the new Imperialism, not yet born. Neither the Evangelicals nor the Liberals held the Empire to be worth, in prestige or glory or money, the risk and cost of retaining it. The imperial idea was at its lowest ebb, not because the Englishman was absorbed in home affairs but because he saw in an Empire much to fear and little to value.

With Regard to the United States

The United States—more remote than imperial, more intimate than foreign—were regarded in 1860 with a curious mixture of kinship and dislike. There can be no doubt that the sense of kinship was present and genuine: the people of the United States were thought of as, to some extent at least, fellow Anglo-Saxons. The one and a half centuries of shared loyalties had ended scarcely more than a long lifetime ago. Now, at a time when it was expected that the other English dominions must go the same way, the original revolt could be considered without bitterness as a natural and necessary stage of growth. Emigration had continued throughout the century, and thousands of English families had brothers or sons extolling the virtues of their new home. Whether in fact this led to better understanding of the United States*—an exceedingly doubtful proposition—it served to strengthen the idea and reality of Anglo-Saxon consanguinity. Withal, there was a hint of pride: the younger son had left home in a huff amidst freely offered predictions of no good end; but, after all, he seemed to be doing rather well, and it reflected quite creditably on the family name.

But, on the other hand, he had picked up some beastly manners.

★ It is said that the lower classes as those principally linked with emigration had, through letters from kinsmen, a truer understanding of the Civil War than the educated. This means, at most, that they knew more of the North. But the emigrant's probable degree of literacy and the confusion of Northern war aims, especially as to slavery, and the average Northerner's dense ignorance of the South, make the 'truer understanding' absurd. And yet historians still say that the lower classes in England knew "rather more than their 'betters' about the United States, as was shown at the time of the Civil War of 1861-1865." [G.M. Trevelyan, *English Social History*, London, 1944, p 583.]

He talked loudly about what he could do in the world—*would* do when he got round to it—and, in general, bragged unconscionably of his strength, size, freedom, and 'destiny', by which he meant domination of the New World. He was not only in fact growing at an unheard-of and alarming rate but was frequently heard to utter bellicose and insulting remarks directed towards Europe in general and England in particular. Moreover, the arrogant boasting about 'destiny' often included, very pointedly, references to Canada. All this did not make for friendliness. England's preparation to bow to the inevitable in the matter of Canadian independence did not extend to a willingness to permit the United States to stretch from the North Pole to the Rio Grande. That river, indeed, was but a reminder of the British failure to persuade the Texans to maintain their independence instead of becoming another of the United States. Altogether, England would have been fonder of this upstart kinsman, America, had he not spoken with such loud boastfulness and shown so many signs of that family acquisitiveness, now out of fashion at home.

Still, by 1860 most of the serious diplomatic difficulties between the two nations were at an end. The troublesome boundary questions—Maine in the east and the threatening Oregon dispute in the far west—had been settled in the time-honoured Anglo-Saxon way of vigorous argument and fair compromise. Great Britain had ceased to oppose United States expansion in California and in the potentially explosive Caribbean area. Instead of the earlier position that any extension of the United States should be viewed with alarm, such expansion was now seen as a civilizing influence which would eventually extend the area of English trade; in fact, there had been "a definite change of policy. . .decided upon in deference to public opinion and after full debate."[8] The England of Evangelicals and free-trade Liberals, opposed to war, unconcerned with safe-guarding the decaying West Indies, interested above all in free trade unimpeded by ancient hostilities, was making its new temper felt.

But, though the possibility of war—very real in the previous decades—had receded and the future seemed fair, scars remained, on both sides, to embitter the relationship. England recalled blustering and agressive statements of United States Presidents, and there was still the danger to Canada. While the Revolutionary War was a thing of the past, the memory of the more recent war in 1812—regarded with some reason as a rather unsporting attack for trivial reasons when England was at death grips with Bonaparte—had been kept alive ever since, not only by United States trumpetings of victory in the actually indecisive affair but also by the continuing friction over the naval right of search. The United States, having gone to war in order to deny such a right, could not abandon their position; and, unfortunately, it was not merely an academic denial. For, since only England actually endeavoured to stamp out the slave trade by stopping suspected slavers on the high seas, the slave-ship masters of all nations flew the United States flag. Thus the Royal Navy was frequently presented with the alternatives of allowing a possible slaver to escape or of risking the diplomatic protests and tension sure to follow if the vessel turned out to be innocent. England could only feel that a noble and generous cause was being blocked by petty pride. In 1858, however, as part of the general new policy with regard to the United States, she abandoned the disputed right of search, and in 1860 it was of no more importance than the other settled but not quite forgotten issues. Its significance for us lies in its effect on public opinion a year later when it was an *English* vessel that was boarded and searched; and also in its contribution to the wartime doubt of the genuineness of Northern opposition to slavery.

Naval rights on the high seas were of less concern in the year 1860 than the challenge to the English mercantile marine. About a decade earlier they had begun to appear: slim, fine-bowed ships with incredibly lofty canvas, racing at speeds up to 21 knots over the trade routes of the seas 'with moonsails at the main'—the Baltimore and Yankee Clippers. England's lead in carrying the world's choice cargoes was threatened, at least until her own superb clippers, *Cutty Sark* and her sisters, slid down the ways. But the splendour of these lovely ships was to be short-lived. The day of the iron steamship was already at hand; and by 1862 the Confederate cruisers were sailing from England to do their duty. Inasmuch as this was handsomely done and resulted in virtually the whole United States mercantile fleet's being sunk or tied up to rot in their harbours, it is not altogether to be wondered at if there were a few subdued cries of "Well done!" from the quays of Liverpool and London.

Except for the rivalry at sea, real commercial competition from the United States had scarcely been thought of. Economically, the United States were regarded mainly as a market and, more particularly, as a source of raw materials including wheat and tobacco and, above all, cotton. The utter dependence on the Southern cotton-planters, who grew over four-fifths and all the best of the cotton England imported, was a source of anxiety to a few far-sighted men; for upon these cotton manufactures, whose annual value exceeded the national revenue, depended directly or indirectly around a fifth of the population.[9] This vital industry—larger by a third than the combined cotton industries of all Europe and the United States—rested so completely upon the cotton crops of the South that well before the war Englishmen were warning that such dependence— "constitutes the structural weakness, the feet of clay of our otherwise gigantic commercial power.... The entire failure of a cotton crop, should it ever occur, would utterly destroy, and perhaps forever, all the manufacturing prosperity we possess.... the misfortune would involve this country in a series of calamities, politically, socially, and commercially such as cannot be contemplated without anxiety and dismay."[10]

Although a few men were aware of the dangers of such dependence, far more were aware of the United States' stubborn and annoying refusal to see the benign light of free trade that shone upon so much of the world. The United States were, in fact, the chief obstacle to the complete triumph of that principle; but

Englishmen saw some hope in the Southern states which, selling the bulk of their products to Europe and wishing to buy the cheaper manufactured goods of England, preferred the 'principle of progress' to the protection of New England industry. The history of Southern complaints against protection, culminating in South Carolina's threat of 'nullifying' a tariff, is the history of a genuine grievance, which England was soon to discover, seeing in it somewhat more perhaps than was there.

Although England and the South were economically complementary, the friendly sentiments that might have followed from the fact were checked in England by Southern slavery, in the South by English abolitionism. It is difficult to be sure of what Englishmen really thought in 1860 about the United States or of what distinction, if any, was made between the North and the South. The books of travellers are often slanted in harmony with a particular political bias—generally either that more democracy in England would be undesirable and therefore the democratic United States and all their works must be discredited, or that more democracy at home was precisely what was wanted and therefore the doings of the transatlantic Utopia must be eulogized. Since those fortifying the former position were more apt to be wealthy enough to travel, most of the books stress the boorishness of 'Jonathan', the corruption of his governments, and the merriment to be found in the spectacle of such a tobacco-chewing ignoramus's attempting to govern himself. Apart from travellers, there were Englishmen who never mentioned the United States without a sneer; others who never mentioned them at all; and then there were Messrs Cobden and Bright who beyond doubt praised them to a wearisome degree. "Look," said these latter, "at the Model Republic,—behold its unbroken prosperity, the harmony of its people under the system of universal suffrage, the lightness of its taxation,—behold, above all, its immunity from war!"* This tendency to see across the Atlantic a beacon to lead

---

* Goldwin Smith, *England & America,* A Lecture, Manchester, 1865, p 12. Smith, who also admired the U.S. & eventually went there to live, is presumably epitomizing, with mild irony, his colleagues' prewar talk.

the English barque into harbour or a lighthouse warning her off
the shoals suggests that at least the more articulate Englishmen saw
in the Republic—as in truth they had always done—exactly what
they wanted to see.

So far we have merely discovered that, while some Englishmen
liked the United States, others did not. The distinction between the
North and the South is equally difficult to determine. A moral line
was drawn between the states where slavery was forbidden and those
where it was not, but the line was a little blurred by the Yankee
slave-trader as well as by reports of the treatment of the Negro in
the North. Nevertheless, Evangelical England roundly condemned
the Southerners and warmly supported the New England aboli-
tionists. *Uncle Tom's Cabin* had appeared in England in 1852 and
a million copies in numerous editions—including a 'non-evangelical
edition'—were sold in a twelvemonth.[11] There can be little doubt
that this vivid, emotional novel by 'the little woman who made the
great war'★ firmly established the South's moral guiltiness in the
minds of many Englishmen (as it had done in the minds of many
previously uncommitted Northerners), and not only guilt but abiding
if hardly representative prototypes of the Planter, the Overseer, and
the miserable, freedom-loving Slave. No other transatlantic author
presented his country so effectively to England, although several
touched upon the theme that was often to be heard during the war:
the money-grubbing Northerners and, by contrast, "the aristocracy
of the Southern States, founded on birth and education".[12] The
great source book of ideas about America, the most authoritative
and, in fact, the most penetrating, was still Alexis de Tocqueville's
De la démocratie en Amérique, published in two parts in 1835 and
1840, in which years, also, the English translation, *Democracy in
America,* was published. No one who read this book could dismiss
the American democratic experiment as less than significant, and
both those who hated democracy and those who loved it could find

★ So Lincoln is supposed to have addressed Mrs. Stowe during the war.

much in de Tocqueville to support their positions. Certain English
writers, particularly Charles Dickens with *Martin Chuzzlewit,* probably had considerable influence in fixing certain unflattering ideas
about the United States; but, since Dickens' experiences were chiefly
in the North, these ideas in his case are related to the generally
Yankee type of 'Jonathan'. While the importance of *Martin
Chuzzlewit* in shaping opinion has often been remarked, it is seldom,
if at all, remembered that a decade later came Thackeray's *Esmond.*
Despite the fact that it deals with the England of Queen Anne's
time, it is still Virginia that the gallant Colonel chooses for his
retirement, and in the final pages Col. Esmond speaks of the idyllic
country-house life and the happy darkies of his new Castlewood
in that land. Still more significant, Thackeray's *The Virginians* was
published serially in the two years just prior to 1860, and dealt with
two young Virginian gentlemen of the late eighteenth century moving
in the loftiest English society. These fine gentlemen, belonging to
a great Virginian house, fond of England and thoroughly English,
opposed to the slave trade but keeping their jolly and contented
'servants', may well have prepared the way for a change in the views
of the 'educated million' two or three years later. Here is
Thackeray—an *English* writer of honour and distinction who, clearly, was serving no special interest—on the Old Dominion of
Virginia:—

> The old usages of Virginia, indeed, were fondly modelled after
> the English customs. It was a loyal colony. The Virginians
> boasted that King Charles II. had been king in Virginia before
> he had been king in England. English king and English church
> were alike faithfully honoured there. The resident gentry were
> allied to good English families. They held their heads above
> the Dutch traders of New York, and the money-getting Round-
> heads of Pennsylvania and New England. Never were people
> less republican than those of the great province which was soon
> to be foremost in the memorable revolt against the British
> Crown. The gentry of Virginia dwelt on their great lands after
> a fashion almost patriarchal.... Their ships took the tobacco

off their private wharves on the banks of the Potomac or the James river, and carried it to London or Bristol,—bringing back English goods and articles of home manufacture in return for the only produce which the Virginian gentry chose to cultivate.... To be the proprietor of black servants shocked the feelings of no Virginian gentlemen; nor, in truth, was the despotism exercised over the negro race generally a savage one. The food was plenty; the poor black people lazy and not unhappy. You might have preached negro emancipation to Madam Esmond of Castlewood as you might have told her to let the horses run loose out of her stables; she had no doubt but that the whip and the corn-bag were good for both.[13]

"After all," the English reader may have thought after reading this, "if these were the Virginians who followed General Washington, if these were Southerners at the close of the eighteenth century, they will not have turned into 'Jonathan' by the middle of the nineteenth: there must, therefore, be two Americas." It will be worth while to compare this idea of the South, in due course, with some of the war-time descriptions.

But the reader of Thackeray and Dickens and the reader of nothing were alike in one respect, their dense ignorance of the United States. Sir Leslie Stephen wrote that in 1860: "The name of America... called up to the ordinary English mind nothing but a vague cluster of associations, compounded of Mrs. Trollope, *Martin Chuzzlewit,* and *Uncle Tom's Cabin.* A few flying reminiscences of disputes about territory, and a few commonplaces about democracy, made up what we were pleased to call our opinions."[14] The Englishman of 1860 had not the knowledge that would make intelligible the situation soon to burst upon him. Indeed, his interest was at a minimum. In that year, with a significance he could not have appreciated had he known, the South shipped to English mills a record cotton crop; and with an equally great and then-unintelligible significance, Southerners were continuing to spurn any Northern or English suggestions that Dickens might be the equal of their beloved Scott—prophet of the chivalric and militant ideal they sought to live.[15]

With Regard to Foreign Affairs

One thing only needs to be said of British foreign policy in 1860: it was the policy then, as throughout the century, of maintaining the balance of power in Europe and the preponderance of power on the seas. The latter was menaced in the Mediterranean by Russian conquest of Turkey: consequently England fought the Crimean War. While there were other good reasons for the war no doubt, there were good reasons at different times to fight most of the European nations—but this was the only Continental war after Waterloo. It is not necessary to examine the other causes; probably there is truth in the comment by the editor of *The Times:* "The country took to the Crimean war because it was so long since we had enjoyed that luxury...it had paid so many millions a year so many years for its army and wanted the natural equivalent in glory."[16] There was, in truth, little glory won there, except by the Light Brigade and Florence Nightingale; but the country could take pride in them. The point is, England *did* enjoy her luxury, had got some measure of glory, and was in 1860, therefore, no longer languishing, if ever she did, for the want of them. Any further desire for military adventure that could exist in Evangelical, Bethamite England was satisfied by the skilful suppression of the Indian Mutiny in 1857 and by the expeditions against China in 1858 and in 1860 itself.

In the latter year England's attitude towards the major powers was one of suspicion if not dislike. In the almost-great year of 1848, with liberal ideas everywhere ascendant, a number of countries had taken short but earnest steps towards freedom and constitutional government, only to fail and lapse into the ancient despotism. In France an emperor (only in retrospect a somewhat comic-opera figure) suggested the old imperial dream—and he bore the dread name of

Napoleon. After the Crimean War, this bearded emperor with the sombre eyes was the strongest—and most unpredictable—of the European powers. England did not trust him, although in fact Napoleon wanted the friendship of England. Russia was the recent enemy, and her designs on Turkey and even, eventually, India were suspect. Prussia was rather undervalued, by England as well as Napoleon. There was no love for Spain, and less for Austria, the oppressor of Italy.

If England's distrust of the often-cooperative Napoleon is relevant to this study, her sympathy for struggling Italy is more so. The word 'liberal' in 1860 still suggested more freedom, not less. The name of England was a name of hope for men and women fighting to be free. In the early years of the century Shelley wrote impassioned poetry in support of Naples against Austria; Lord Byron died for Hellas. English Liberalism established Greece, supported the Spanish colonies against their masters, and secured Belgian independence. No matter if motives other than pure love of liberty entered in— when was there ever a crusade of pure, unsullied idealism?—the love of liberty was there too, and England had got a name for helping suppressed nationalities, a name that rang with splendour in her own ears as well as European. And Lord Palmerston was that England, as Canning had been before him, as Gladstone was to be after him. And in 1860, not long after England had rescued the Turk from Russia, her attention was fixed on Italy. Garibaldi and the Thousand were freeing Sicily, and Englishmen were watching with passionate enthusiasm. Public subscriptions were taken, and the red-shirted captain was hailed as the very figure of freedom wrestling with ancient tyranny. Meanwhile, the 'Triumvirate' were working together with matchless skill, aided by fortune, to secure the future of the new Italy.

The England of 1860 was prepared to fight in the event of a real threat to the European balance of power or to the English preponderance of power on the seas; but at the moment there was no such threat—nor was the war between the American states to

threaten either of the two paramount interests. Doubts continued
to be entertained of Napoleon, only partly allayed by his professions
of friendship. No one, though, was much alarmed. England was im-
pregnable and everyone knew it. Secure and prosperous at home,
Englishmen displayed their deep-rooted attachment to the cause of
freedom by ardour for the cause of Italy.

A British expeditionary force was operating against Pekin. The
Prince of Wales was travelling in America. An obscure westerner
named Lincoln became in November the President-elect, and there
seemed to be some equally obscure bickering about it. This was scarcely to be wondered at, in a democracy.

This chapter has been an essay in seeing, an effort to pin the moment down and have a look at 1860 before it merges into the sixties
and is lost in Victorian England. We must move on now into
1861—from 1860. The transatlantic news came by clipper and nor-
mally it arrived a fortnight after the event. The ocean cable had
broken two years earlier, not to be mended for another six years.
The clipper that left the United States shortly after the 20th of
December had favouring winds for she arrived in the Thames estuary
on the 31st. And in the mails she brought was the news of an event—
the decisive reaction to the election of Abraham Lincoln: On the
last day of the year 1860 England learned that the sovereign state
of South Carolina had formally seceded from the union of states
she had helped to create.★

★ If South Carolina was not sovereign, she at least believed that she was, nor
  was any other state certain she was not. If she lost the rights of sovereignty
  by the judgement of war four years later, perhaps that judgement is not
  retroactive.

[1] G.M. Young, Ed., *Early Victorian England 1830-1865,* 2 vol., London, [1934], v II, p 414. [Hereafter: G.M. Young]

[2] Lord Tennyson, "Locksley Hall".

[3] Louis Blanc, *Letters on England,* Second Series, 2 vol., London, 1867, vol. I, pp 55 & 120. (N.B. There are also his *Letters on England,* 2 vol., London, 1866—four volumes altogether.) [Hereafter: Louis Blanc; or Louis Blanc, 2nd Series] The *Letters* (translated from the French) were written by M. Blanc for papers in France, and for that reason are particularly valuable in their detached account of English sentiments.

[4] D.C. Somervell, *English Thought in the Nineteenth Century,* New York, 1929, p 182. (Sir F. Rogers, Permanent Under-Secy., 1860-71.)

[5] J.A. Roebuck, *The Colonies of England,* London, 1849, pp 188 & 189.

[6] Quoted by G.M. Young, v II, p 394.

[7] Quoted by George McHenry, *The Cotton Trade: its Bearing upon the Prosperity of Great Britain, &c.,* London, 1863, pp 75-76.

[8] *The Cambridge History of British Foreign Policy:* vol II 1815-1866, Cambridge, 1923, p 282.

[9] E.L. Woodward, *The Age of Reform 1815-1870,* Oxford, [1949], p 300.

[10] Quoted by F.L. Owsley, *King Cotton Diplomacy,* Chicago, [1931], p 11. [Hereafter: Owsley] (Also quoted, with variations, by the C.S. pamphleteer, Col. T. Jordan, in *The South: its Products, Commerce, & Resources,* London, 1861.)

[11] H.G. Nicholas, *"Uncle Tom's Cabin* 1852-1952", *History Today,* II (June, 1952)6, p 418.

[12] F.J. Grund, *Aristocracy in America,* 2 vol., London, 1839, v II, p 25.

[13] W.M. Thackeray, *The Virginians,* Chap. III (pp 20-21, 1891 edit., London).

[14] 'L.S.' [Sir Leslie Stephen], *The "Times" on the American War: A Historical Study,* London, 1865, pp 4-5.

[15] R.G. Osterweis, *Romanticism & Nationalism in the Old South,* New Haven, 1949, p 43 & also pp 213-214.

[16] *The Times (History),* p 373.

Chapter Two

The Events of 1861

This England—a country with strong sentiments on free trade and slavery and self-determination—was faced early in 1861, and increasingly throughout the year, with the necessity of taking a position on the striking events in her former dominions. "Never, within my memory," wrote an Oxford don a few years later, "have the hearts of Englishmen been so deeply moved by any foreign struggle... —not even, if I recollect aright, by the Indian mutiny or by our war with Russia."[1] This chapter is mainly an account of their initial apathy becoming a deepening interest and their gradual development of a coherent position. Although they—the Englishmen that are 'England's opinion'—will appear to change their sympathies in the course of this year, we shall see that their first attitude, based upon inadequate knowledge, was as inevitable and consistent with their beliefs as the later position they assumed when further light fell upon the confusion in America.

The First Position

Hard upon the heels of South Carolina followed the other states of the 'Deep South'—out of the Union that they considered merely a compact among sovereign states. Their citizens serving in the federal forces or legislative assembly resigned. Property used for federal purposes—forts and post offices—was resumed by the states. By February these states had associated themselves in a new 'united nations', the Confederate States of America, headed by President Jefferson Davis, who immediately sent diplomatic representatives to Washington and Europe. These envoys were, respectively, to request the return of two forts still occupied by United States forces, and the diplomatic recognition of the Confederate States. Thus peacefully, with marked legality of form and propriety of manner, appeared a new nation. There ensued a lull, a waiting on the Lincolnian unknown quantity.

The reaction of England to all of this was confused. The Government undoubtedly remarked that a former aim of their diplomacy—keeping Texas independent—was now rather more than achieved. It is quite possible that an earlier government, in accordance with the policy of opposing United States growth, might promptly have recognized and if necessary supported the Confederacy; the Government of 1861 did not. Englishmen in general, who had often heard predictions of the ultimate dissolution of the Union, now saw it happening—in, they noted with approval, a peaceful manner. The constitutional issue of the legality of secession, which even those who lived under the Constitution could not decide except by force, was one upon which few Englishmen then had even an opinion. They knew two facts: that slavery had something, perhaps all, to do with the quarrel; and that nearly all of the cotton-growing states were in the new Confederacy. On the former they founded a general sympathy for the bereft United States. Defeat in a Presidential election seemed an inadequate if not unsporting reason for quitting the Union—it was noted that half the Southern states had remained in it—and, if there was a deeper reason, it could only be a Northern intention of putting down slavery, with which England would be bound to sympathize. And on the latter of the two facts they based their urgent hope that there would be no war. "Let them go!" said England to the North in newspaper leading articles and speeches. "Let them go! They are really not worth keeping—certainly not worth fighting over. You are still a huge country—you have the best of America—and now that you have got rid of those hot-headed slave-owners, perhaps you will be able to put an end to slavery in your own states. At all events, do not have a war which would make it worse for the slaves and be ruinous to trade." The old hostility to the United States was, for the moment, concentrated upon the Confederate States. But Englishmen were still not very interested in the obscure quarrel; it would take war to make them so.

In March Lincoln took office and—in his most important words of the war for Englishmen—stated unequivocally:

> I have no purpose, directly or indirectly to interfere with the institution of slavery in the States where it exists. I believe I have no lawful right to do so, and I have no inclination to do so.

One month later Lincoln made the decision for war—war to save the Union, war to compel the Southern states to submit to the government of a sovereign *nation*. He ordered, against the advice of his Cabinet and commanding general, an expedition for the relief of Fort Sumter in the harbour of Charleston, South Carolina. The expedition had no chance of success, but it was not intended to be successful. The truce was ended. As Lincoln had known they must do, the Confederate States reduced the fort. The North had a perfect *casus belli:* the South had fired on the Flag. Lincoln called for troops. Two days later Virginia, followed by her sister states, withdrew from the Union.

In England the first doubts of the justice of the Northern cause appeared. Lincoln's inaugural address appeared to confirm with finality the statements of others that slavery was *not* the issue. The North, then, need not automatically be supported. Furthermore, whatever the cause of the original secession, the case of Virginia was manifestly different. ★ The very "accession of her splendid and

★ If in these pages it sometimes appears that the Southern cause was mainly upheld by Virginia, it is because she and South Carolina were best known in the beginning by England, and Virginia even more so after the emergence of Lee & Jackson and the great battles on Virginian fields.

powerful name to the roll of the Confederate States'', in the words of the Marquess of Lothian, and "the unanimous resolve of those States to transfer their common capital from Montgomery to Richmond''[2] tended to dispel the idea, urged by the North, that the seceding states were in the grip of a few lawless conspirators. Moreover, not only was Virginia's reason for secession—Lincoln's use of force, unauthorized by the Constitution (and, indeed, rejected by the drawers of that document), against a state—not only was this very high ground with a strong appeal to Englishmen but the Virginian secession on such high ground tended to sanction the preceding withdrawals.

Still, all of this was not at once clear, and confusions of all sorts preplexed the situation. There were doubts of Northern motives and doubts, even after Fort Sumter, whether there would be a war. Lincoln's proclamation of a blockade had been correctly answered by the Queen's proclamation of neutrality. Although United States troops had invaded Virginia one day after her citizens voted to confirm her ordinance of secession and confused fighting was reported, Seward, the Northern Secretary of State—widely regarded as the 'Prime Minister' or effective power—continued to assert that ninety days would see the rebellion at an end since it was caused by a handful of conspirators in an otherwise loyal South. There is a vast difference between the uprising of a determined people and a treasonable conspiracy: as long as the latter was asserted and remained a possibility, Englishmen continued to sympathize with the North, as the side of law and order. But the letters of W.H. Russell, the very able correspondent of *The Times* in America, suggested a united and resolute Confederacy—and if this were the case, it was generally believed, the Northern effort would be futile. The first English reaction had been reproaches for the South; now there was an anxious desire to persuade the North to let the seceded states go without a useless war. When the North unreasonably persisted despite such good advice, England's third reaction would be anger at headstrong Northern pride. A growing number of Englishmen were discovering parallels and, not unreasonably, viewing the affair as George III and the Thirteen Colonies all over again. In July a leading article in *The Times* pointed out that only the Southern states "were able to celebrate Independence Day with unmixed feelings."[3] If England had had to swallow the bitter dose, why not the United States? Also about this time, the argument began to be advanced that the Northern tariff was the real cause of secession—an argument bound to appeal to free-trading England and destined to become an article of faith for many Englishmen.

The Correction of the Position

In the latter part of July the United States army moved into Virginia to crush the rebellion, and Congressmen and even wives went along to see it crushed. Near the little village of Manassas on the stream called Bull Run they found the Confederate army. Battle was joined. At times the issue seemed in doubt. But at a critical moment the Virginian troops stood fast, and a Confederate officer shouted to his own retreating men: "There stands Jackson, like a stone wall. Rally behind the Virginians!" Perhaps it was the turning point. In a few more hours the United States army, ceasing to be a disciplined force, sped back to Washington in a panic rout, the Congressmen bounding along far in front.

The news of this first major battle arrived in early August and, after England had read W.H. Russell's vivid account of the Northern army's flight, there was a marked decrease in sympathy for the Union and an equally marked increase for the South. Those who had believed Seward's assurance that the South was really loyal to the United States now "got new lights, and found that the South, instead of a reluctant people, whose political wishes were overridden by ambitious individuals, was an unanimous and enthusiastic community, resolved to fight for, and live under, a government of their own choice, separate from the Northern States. This new light produced a complete revulsion of feeling in England.'''[4] It was not only the discovery that the Southerners were in deadly earnest about wanting their freedom that threw new light into the transatlantic obscurity, although that made a tremendous difference; it was also the dawn of a genuine liking for the South. Justin McCarthy, after describing the early unanimity for the North and the view of the Confederates as turbulent and troublesome fellows, thus wrote of the effect of the battle:

> Suddenly, as if to decide wavering minds, an event was reported which made hosts of admirers for the South in England.... [The news] was received by vast numbers with exultation, and with derision at the expense of the 'Yankees.' It had been well settled that the Yankees were hypocrites and low fellows before; but now it came out that they were mere runaways and cowards. The English people, for a brave nation, are surprisingly given to accusing their neighbours of cowardice. They have a perfect mania for discovering cowardice all over the world. Napoleon was a coward to a past generation; the French were for a long time cowards; the Italians were cowards;...the Russians still are cowards. In 1861 the Yankees were the typical cowards of the earth. A very flame of enthusiasm leaped up for the brave South, which though so small in numbers had contrived with such spirit and ease to defeat the Yankees.[5]

There were no further battles for half a year with the exception of a small Confederate victory at Ball's Bluff. England's conviction of Northern pusillanimity and Southern valour had time to become fixed almost unshakeably; nor was there, indeed, much reason to alter this conviction with the advent of Lee and Jackson to the Southern command.

The half year after the battle was not uneventful, though; for in November of 1861, a United States warship stopped the British mail packet *Trent* on the high seas, searched her, and forcibly removed two passengers, J.M. Mason, Virginian, and John Slidell, Louisianian, Confederate Commissioners to London and Paris, respectively. This act—to Englishmen, this high-handed insult—struck England like a thunderbolt. "There never was within memory such a burst of feeling... The people are frantic with rage, and were the country polled, I fear 999 men out of a thousand would declare for immediate war."[6] Englishmen suddenly remembered all their old irritation in connexion with the slave trade:[7] it seemed that the United States, after piously denying the right of naval search to the point of blocking the great humanitarian cause of destroying the slave trade, were now, when it suited their purpose, proving themselves hypocrites by exercising that right—and against an *English* ship! Anger swept across the country: "public opinion was on fire. The Clubs overflowed with visitors animated by a sort of thrilling curiosity. ... In the general indignation there was mingled something of a haughty astonishment. What! England insulted on her own grand domain, the sea! And to make matters worse, the challengers were those Americans from whose hands England had had for years past to swallow so many affronts!... 'Well!' [said my clergyman acquaintance,] 'my vote is for war, and I would gladly be the first to shoulder a musket. Quite long enough have those bullies been threatening us. There must be an end to it!'"[8] The Ministry drafted a stiff ultimatum to the United States and prepared for war. The Navy was put in a state of readiness. Several thousand troops were ordered to Canada. The Guards embarked under the impression they were bound for Charleston to fight alongside the Southerners, and the regimental band mingled 'Dixie' and 'I am off for Charleston' with the 'British Grenadiers' and 'God Save the Queen'.[9]

By a hairsbreadth, it seems, war was averted. The Government's ultimatum couched in language so severe that the United States could only have chosen war was slightly toned down by the dying Prince Consort. Even then Washington might have found itself swept into war by the popular enthusiasm which was causing gold medals to be struck for the officer who had stopped the *Trent* but for the fact that the Atlantic cable was broken, and thus there was time for second thoughts in America. Actually the North had no choice, for it would have been madness to embark on a war with Great Britain while still hoping to conquer the South. Shortly after the end of the year, it became known that the United States had surrendered the Confederate Commissioners and there would be no war. Thus the year came to an end. England and the Confederacy had not become allies, but large numbers of Englishmen, no longer bored by the happenings in America, were Southern allies in sentiment.

The Permanent Position

The Ministry did not bring on a war as they undoubtedly could have done. Once more, in the autumn of the following year, 1862, they were to come very close to decisive action; then never again. We shall later have occasion to consider that crisis and why the 'Triumvirate' did not act: otherwise the war on the governmental and diplomatic level—Seward's threats and bombast, Lord John Russell's hesitations, the duel between the Virginian Mason and the American Adams (as they might have described themselves)—has little relevancy to English sympathy for the South. Similarly, except in so far as they affect the sympathy, we shall not be concerned with the war on the economic and propaganda levels. The Confederacy was convinced, as were many Englishmen, that cotton hunger would force England to intervene—"Better fight the Yankees than starve the operatives...The American Blockade must be broken",[10] said a leader in *Reynolds's Newspaper,* 29th September 1861—but King Cotton did not rule. Because of this conviction, the Confederacy waited until late in the war to attempt to organize mass opinion, as the United States were doing; and the attempt was too late to affect the issue. But powerful friends of the South in England, controlling or having access to most of the journals, did effectively present the Confederate case over and over again. A Confederate, Henry Hotze, ably edited *The Index,* a journal that served as an authoritative and trustworthy source of Southern news and interpretations. Distinguished Southerners—such as Captain Matthew Maury, C.S.N.—moved among the great country houses, presenting the Confederate case to willing listeners. Because there were so many forces at work upon English opinion, especially educated opinion, there is no way to gauge the effect of any one of them. But it seems probable that the chief effect of all of them was to clarify the issues involved in the war and to correct some of the rather remarkable distortions of the United States press.

England became 'Southern' after the battle of Manassas (Bull Run) and the *Trent* affair, and remained so to the end.★ Events served but to strengthen and confirm this position. The first period of the war, from the English point of view, may be said to end with the taking of this permanent position. The subsequent periods, although even more eventful, concern us less, for the convictions of Englishmen with regard to the war only deepened. The earlier half of 1862 was a period of further confusion as to the military situation: the huge and indecisive battle of Shiloh in the west, a dramatic but again indecisive duel between the Confederate ironclad *Virginia* and the Federal ironclad *Monitor,* the fall of New Orleans to the Union Navy, and the massive army of McClellan moving slowly and ominously upon Richmond. English hostility to the North grew stronger.

Then Robert E. Lee, who had declined the command of the United States Army at the outbreak of hostilities, took command of the Confederate Army of Northern Virginia and swept McClellan out of Virginia. This battle, known as the Seven Days, won the South

---

★ The reader is reminded of the meaning of 'England' (see pp 15-16 above). As to what proportion of Englishmen constituted the England that became Southern, see Chapter IV.

hosts of admirers; with it the third period begins, July 1862 to July 1863, when a great tide of Southern victory lapped at the frontiers of the Union. Then from the loss of Gettysburg and Vicksburg in 1863 through a year and a half, it was for England, *not* the period of defeat but that of strategic withdrawals. And then on the last day of 1864, when England learned that the United States General Sherman had burned his way through the heart of the Confederacy to the sea, the final period began: then, and *only* then, did Englishmen believe that the South was going down; and in four months it was gone.

Only the first period, embracing all of 1861 from the secession of South Carolina to the surrender of the Confederate Commissioners by Washington, was marked by real change in England. The country developed, from virtually none, a most intense interest. Sympathy extended to the United States, on the grounds that they were trying to free the slaves, was withdrawn when it was discovered that they were not trying to free the slaves but only to compel the Southern states to return. Dislike of the South as treasonable conspirators became liking for a resolute people. England, then— believing in the right of a people to determine their own government, deploring wars of reconquest, and admiring bravery—could not consistently withhold her sympathy from the South; and she did not.

[1] Goldwin Smith, *op.cit.*, p 10.

[2] W.S.R. Kerr, 8th Marquess of Lothian, *The Confederate Secession,* London & Edinburgh, 1864, p 159. [Hereafter: LOTHIAN]

[3] *The Times (History),* p 362.

[4] Stephen Locke, *English Sympathies & Opinions Regarding the Late American Civil War,* London, 1866, pp 7-8. [Hereafter: Locke]

[5] Justin McCarthy, v III, pp 296-297.

[6] E.D. Adams, quoting a Londoner, v I, p 217.

[7] See above, pp 22.

[8] Louis Blanc, v I, pp 209-210.

[9] T.L. Harris, *The Trent Affair,* Indianapolis, [1896], p 144.

[10] Quoted by Henry Pelling, *America & the British Left,* London, [1956], p 7 fn.

Part II Flood

Chapter Three

The English Gentlemen of the South

Chapter Four

The Southern Gentlemen of England

Chapter Three

The English Gentlemen of the South

Passing from the springs of English sympathy for the Confederacy, we have now to examine the sympathy at flood. We must, before considering its extent, first look at the tributary streams that combined to create the flood. For all of the English friends of the South did not speed her arms for the same reason. The Southern Cross—battle flag of the embattled Confederacy—sprang forward or staggered back, and they cheered or went about with long faces. But some were cheering another blow at the Republic and some another blow for free trade, while some were simply cheering General Lee. There were men to whom free trade meant primarily their own or England's gain, and others to whom free trade was a panacea for the ills of the whole world. There were women who hated and dreaded the encroachments of Northern democracy, and women who, more simply, extended their sympathy to that which was gracious and courteous in the South. And so with the other reasons. It is not well to dismiss the adherents of any cause with contemptuous allegations of insincerity and selfishness. We can do so with none of the groups that followed with their hopes or prayers the fortunes of the Southern Cross.

The Golden Dream

The Southern states had scarcely separated themselves from the

Northern when two events occurred, almost simultaneously: The
United States Senate, after fourteen Southern Members had
withdrawn, passed with a majority of eleven votes the almost pro-
hibitive Morrill Tariff; the Confederate States adopted a Constitution forbidding *any* tariff except for revenue—a denial, that is, of
the principle of protection. Thus from the economic point of view,
which to some students of history is almost the only point of view,
a major issue became perfectly clear. The North stood for protection; the South for free trade. And for Englishmen—those, at least,
who believed in free trade, or realized not only the specific
dependence of the English mills upon Confederate cotton but also
the complementary relationship of the two economies—certain con-
clusions were obvious. "This [tariff] was the first use the North
made of its victory [in the Senate]",[1] said one Englishman in a pamphlet, and again: "If the South wins, I fancy I can descry glimmer-
ing on the horizon...free trade with a boundless expanse of the
richest soil, from which English mills and English ships will reap
a golden harvest".[2] The contrast between North and South was real
and unambiguous, and so too were England's free-trade convictions.

With those convictions and after these events, it was natural that
many Englishmen, particularly Radicals of the Manchester School
such as Richard Cobden, should readily embrace the theory of the
South's seceding because of economic oppression—since there *had*
to be a reason for secession and both sides agreed that slavery was
not the reason. The theory did not, in fact, reach the heart of the
matter (no more did slavery), but there was enough truth in it to
make it persuasive. As one of the ablest of the 'Southern'
Englishmen, James Spence, said, the South had long been convinced
"that the Union was worked to the profit of the North and their
own loss. All who are familiar with Southern literature know it to
be full of bitterness on this topic; and when you consider that the
immediate cause of the revolt of those thirteen colonies from this
country was a duty of 3d. per lb. on tea..."[3]—considered so, it
all appeared very logical. A great many Englishmen were convinced

and remained convinced.

The Confederate States were well aware of the appeal of economic facts. Their Secretary of State instructed James Mason on his mission to England to stress the free-trade commitment of his Government, as well as the British people's "deep political and commercial interest in the establishment of the independence of the Confederate States".[4] Similarly, the Southern Independence Association of London, a group of English sympathizers, said in their *Address to the Public* that England's "best interests will be promoted by creating a direct trade with a people so enterprising as the Confederates, inhabiting a land so wide and so abundant in the richest gifts of Providence, and anxious to place themselves in immediate connection with the manufacturers and consumers of Europe."[5]

Such appeals became imperative in the anxiety caused by the cotton 'famine' and the suffering of the Lancashire cotton operatives. The 'King Cotton' doctrine of the Confederates—that England would have to intervene in order to keep her economy from collapsing from want of cotton—seemed to be proving its validity. Half a million working-class people were dependent upon charity; efforts to obtain sufficient cotton from India and elsewhere were unavailing. But King Cotton was deposed before his reign began by forces that neither Southerners nor Englishmen could have foreseen. The great crop of 1860, and large earlier crops, had caused overproduction; for the manufacturers the war came as a timely intervention of Fate to save them from the ruinous consequences of the enormous glut of cotton goods. Far from suffering, the mill owners were helped if not saved by the war and rather hoped—so long as the operatives remained quiescent—it would continue. Apart from King Cotton's ineffectiveness, there were certain other circumstances tending to reduce the imperative of the economic appeal. The CSS *Alabama* and her sister cruisers were engaged in sinking the 'Yankee' mercantile marine; if the war but continued 'one more year' they would all be sunk—to the great advantage of the English shipowners. The linen and woollen manufactures were booming as they had not done since the rise of cotton. The Confederate States were buying all the vessels to be had; and both of the combatants were buying munitions and supplies of all sorts, to the value of some twenty million pounds.[6] The owners of these manufactures had much reason to be grateful to the South but also much reason not to manifest their gratitude by any action tending to stop the war.

Nevertheless, there were many Englishmen, including some of these owners, who took a longer view, preferring unlimited cotton in the future to immediate war profits, free trade with the Confederacy to doing business through New York. They did not miss the implications of an M.P.'s statement in the House "that one may read in Boston and other Northern towns, over the doors of certain shops: 'No English goods sold here;' and...that at Richmond a member of the Confederate Government had said to him: 'We look upon England as our workshop.'"[7] These men who looked into the future, seeing the Confederacy as the natural complement to their own economy, dreamed of a day when "London may...occupy the position which New York has hitherto held in regard to the South",[8] yet they felt it necessary to warn their countrymen that: "the prospective alliance of the South is not a thing with which we can afford to play at pitch-and-toss....in offering our hand to the South, we shall wipe out the old score against us of the half of the former Union, and of that half, too, which is agricultural, and not manufacturing;...Now, is this an alliance we can afford to overlook or to depreciate? Is this one we should allow to slip out of our fingers?"[9]

It was a fine dream from their point of view, and from the South's as well; and it was based on economic realities. Over and over the theme was repeated—The United States will never be our friend for they are a rival, while the South is naturally our friend and ally.—in Parliament[10] and in print. Indeed, the economic link between England and the South, as these Englishmen saw it, was stronger and more natural than that between the North and the South. The Southern states, they said, "have no natural connexion with the Northern States, while their connexion with England is naturally one of the strongest mutual inter-dependence. Three-fourths of their annual produce is sent to us. . . This enormous interchange between them and us ought to be effected directly, and not circuitously; but owing to the Federal Union, and to the injurious operation of its Tariff upon the South, it is artificially and unnaturally managed through the intrusive agency of New York and of the Northern States. . . . England and the South gravitate towards each other with the strongest force of commercial attraction. Each has enormous wants, and each desires exactly what the other has to supply. They form one system, and are bound together by interests completely identical."[11]

This is the 'Golden Dream' in the words of the Englishmen who dreamed it; and this is the first—and, perhaps, the least—of the four sets of reasons for sympathy with the Confederacy. It is least simply because England was too prosperous and the future too veiled; it was not a poor man's dream of riches, the sort that can prompt desperate deeds. It did not come true, but it was a fine dream all the same—surpassed only by the more splendid dream, not altogether fantastic, that some of these Englishmen went on to— that the Confederacy would be willing "to return to any political relation to England that England might be willing to form".[12]★

The Tyranny of the Mob

If the elevating and beneficial rule of an aristocracy must end, said Matthew Arnold in 1864, what is to replace it? The answer

★ Cowell, *op.cit.,* is indirectly quoting John Caldwell Calhoun. But see Appendix for evidence, including this in fuller form, that the idea may have been fairly widespread among leading Southerners.

that was so clear to John Bright—the answer summed up in the phrase, 'the Model Republic'—did not satisfy Matthew Arnold after observing American democracy in action, for he continued: "In other words, and to use a short and significant modern expression which everyone understands, what influences may help us to prevent the English people from becoming, with the growth of democracy, *Americanized?*"[13] Two years later when democracy had won its enormous victory an Englishman wrote sadly: "Perhaps an American England may produce a higher average of happiness than the existing system, but it would not be a country for a gentleman".[14] The note of resignation discernible in these remarks was rarely if ever heard in England before the period of Southern defeat; perhaps it will be shown in later pages that it is not unreasonable to suppose that the resignation grew directly and indirectly out of the defeat.

In 1860 democracy—which meant American democracy—was disliked but not considered inevitable. John Bright and his fellows were met by the deep-rooted conviction that a large democracy could not endure. The Model Democracy had not proved itself—and would not. Sooner or later a large democracy must either break up into smaller states or, as France had done, cease to be a democracy. De Tocqueville, himself, had virtually prophesied such a disintegration, and had suggested the possibility of democracy's being followed by despotism.[15]★ Thoughtful Englishmen waited for one or both of these fates to be meted out to the United States—soon, some of them hoped, for democracies, while they lasted, were unpleasant neighbours. So France had been, and so the United States were. The disagreeableness of the latter was manifested mainly in aggressiveness and continual abuse of England. The editor of *The Times,* Delane, wrote privately to Lord John Russell of England's

★ His thought was perhaps based on the Greek 'Wheel of Government' where the 'rule of the many' (polyarchy or democracy) is succeeded by the 'rule of the one' (monarchy or, more precisely, autocracy).

deep and universal anger at "the foul and incessant abuse of the Americans, statesmen, orators and press,"[16] but—although it was the chief irritant—abuse was not the only distasteful feature of democracy. Englishmen marked the wide-spread corruption in political life and, as it seemed to them, the rise of low men to power, while the higher men, unwilling to play the demagogue, were not sought out. Far from seeing the shining light of liberty in this state, subject to and manifesting the will of the sovereign masses, the English critics saw only the unwholesome 'tyranny of the mob'— which to such a worshipper of liberty as Sir John (later, Lord) Acton was the very antithesis of true freedom. But, given time, the United States were bound to break apart, and then an aristocracy or a monarchy would assert its natural right to rule the fragments: all history proved it.

When upon these cheerful speculations broke the fact that two nations stood where one had been, the fulfillment of the prophecy was accepted with calm approval: "that Union...has been found to exceed the utmost possibility of national extension....[It can] no longer act only as a great magnet on the conduct of the Old World".[17] Moreover, gradually, men saw that the other half of the prophecy was also, at least partly, fulfilled: the Confederacy took shape in their eyes as something other than a democracy; there the best men led instead of making money. Henceforth, the American *democracy* meant the North.

It became no less clear to them that the democracy had not changed its nature. Or, rather, it had changed for the worse; the South, therefore, must have acted as a restraining influence, now withdrawn. The "foul and incessant abuse" directed at England— for not sympathizing wholly with the North and condemning wholly the South—seemed to mount to a climax never reached before. "You will never believe it", wrote an Englishman to a Northerner, "But nine-tenths of every difficulty between you and us arises from the feeling here that your Government does not mean to behave like gentlemen to England."[18] After all, men asked themselves, what

have the Northerners ever done to enlist our support? They are not
fighting to free the slaves. Their Prime Minister, Seward, threatens
to make war on us. Their newspapers "are violent, untruthful, scur-
rilous to a degree which we cannot imagine in this orderly old
land."[19] Perhaps, "worst of all. . . is their appetite for throwing the
blame of their misfortune on guiltless England."[20] Similarly, the
long-despised corruption in the Northern democracy seemed to increase; stories of bribery and graft were too common for remark.
"We have no faith in their honour," wrote one Englishman, ex-
pressing a very common opinion: "We know that they consider
honesty as, at best, a 'policy,' not a principle."[21] The foregoing,
though not without much truth, is one-sided—as one-sided as the
Northern Utopia seen by some of the Radicals, or the stainless
legions fighting for the black man seen by some Nonconformists;
but if we would understand the sympathy for the South, we must
see not only the South but the North as the English friends of the
South saw them. The faults in the American democracy which had
caused dislike in the past were now seen to be unchanged: it was
still corrupt at home and abusive to the world. True to its democratic
nature, it had elected a low man to high office: to these Englishmen,
Lincoln with his crude manners and ill-timed jests was the appropriate symbol of the disintegrating Model Republic, the fitting
expression of 'the sovereign rabble'.

The tyranny of the mob, as they so often called it—the 'mob'
that could override every check of constitution, tradition, or
courtesy—that was the very centre of the detestation of democracy.
It must be understood that these Englishmen who dreaded the rule
of the people were, first of all, honestly afraid of it—*they* did not
believe themselves to be selfishly defending privilege—and, secondly,
they made a sharp distinction (which we do not always do) between
freedom and equality, the first of which they often loved whilst
hating the second. * We who live in a world where democracy (or

---

★ See Epilogue on the relationship of freedom and equality.

a parody of democracy beyond the Iron Curtain) is taken for granted, we who do not question that freedom and virtue flourish (or, at least, freedom) in a society ruled by the people—we must make a distinct effort, if we would understand these earlier Englishmen, to see democracy as they saw it. And they could see it in only one place—the United States. And there they thought they saw, not 'the land of the free' but a tyrant, under whom neither individual nor minority rights were safe. Individualistic, educated Englishmen— themselves a minority—saw a tyrant more arbitrary than monarchs, as, indeed, de Tocqueville had seen★, in "that miserable, levelling democracy and universal suffrage which is so rapidly landing the Northern States in a perfectly Assyrian despotism."[22] Such a description was not as fantastic as it sounds; it received much justification from a series of arbitrary arrests and other denials of Constitutional freedoms in the United States. The Constitution "did not stop the way when the members of the Legislature of Maryland were seized in the night, and hurried off to a dungeon. It did not stop the way when the writ of Habeas Corpus was taken away from the whole of the loyal North."[23]★★ Many Englishmen who had

★ Or, at least, more arbitrary than any monarch who must rule under law. In discussing the "tyranny of the majority", de Tocqueville says that the old maxim—the king can do no wrong—is in America applied to the decision of the majority. (De Tocqueville, p 184) The Englishmen who feared this tyranny found much in de Tocqueville to support their fears, though de Tocqueville is far from total condemnation of democracy.

★ ★ It is, perhaps, well to remark that these events did, in fact, happen. Morison & Commager in *The Growth of the American Republic* (N.Y., 1942, v I, pp 699-700) state that Abraham Lincoln was "a dictator from the standpoint of American constitutional law and practice; and even the safety of the Republic cannot justify certain acts committed under his authority. . . . A loyal mayor of Baltimore, suspected of Southern sympathies, was arrested and confined in a fortress for over a year; a Maryland judge who had charged a grand jury to inquire into illegal acts of government officials was set upon by soldiers. . . beaten and dragged bleeding from his bench, and imprisoned. . . ." They cite many other instances. And these deeds were known in England (whereas the somewhat arbitrary acts of President Davis, which Morison & Commager also point out, were not)—known to Englishmen who were often just then having their first real look at America and at democracy.

wavered between admiration and dislike of democracy were now confirmed in the latter. "We have all been amazed at the way in which the North has violated private liberties",[24] wrote one Englishman; while another, James Spence, in what was probably the most widely-read book of the war, *The American Union,* wrote: "When a people look on with acquiescence, whilst the writ of Habeas Corpus is treated with contempt, whilst the police forbid petitions to the Government, in violation of an express right of the Constitution... [when] legislators [are] imprisoned—property confiscated... there is ample evidence that, whatever may have been the love of liberty in other days, it has become a thing of the past."[25] There seemed to Englishmen, even the most scrupulously fair, little to admire in the spectacle of a democratic people at war. A distinguished and life-long republican, George Grote, confessed a few years before his death: "I have outlived my faith in the efficacy of republican government regarded as a check upon the vulgar passions of a majority in a nation, and I recognize the fact that supreme power lodged in their hands *may* be exercised quite as mischievously as by a despotic ruler like the first Napoleon. The conduct of the Northern States, in the late conflict with the Southern States, has led me to this conclusion, though it costs me much to avow it, even to myself."[26] It is essential to any true understanding of those who sided with the South—or, more precisely, sided against the North, because of their dislike of American democracy—to appreciate that they did not regard themselves as opposing the side that stood for liberty. On the contrary, to them the tyranny of the mob was the very negation and death of freedom.

When they turned to the Confederacy that was in arms against the American democracy, they were prepared, solely because it *was* at war with that democracy (or because, also, it too was so roundly abused), to extend their sympathy. But then they remarked, with pleased surprise, that it was making friendly gestures towards England—rather a rarity on that side of the Atlantic. Someone remembered that it had been the present Confederate Commissioner,

Mason, "who made the motion in the Senate, which led to the most graceful act of courtesy which the American government has shown to England for many years, the refitting and return of the Resolute."[27] In the South, it appeared, something like an aristocracy ruled: "there, owing to the large landed proprietors and the conditions of the country, the mob has not the same power. A certain number of the gentry have leisure to study politics as they ought to be studied".[28] The contrast between the heads of the warring states seemed to bear this out: Lincoln, lacking the halo of victory and assassination, seemed little more than a clumsy buffoon compared to the austerely dignified President Davis; there could be small wonder that the South had withdrawn from the Union. Thus the Englishmen who first saw only two halves of a broken democracy in America; and then sided 'against the North' as manifesting most fully the objectionable features of American democracy; finally discovered an admiration and genuine enthusiasm for the South for what it was. ★ The Duke in Disraeli's *Lothair* comments that the Southerner "has the consolation of suffering in a good cause," and adds: "I look upon an American gentleman with large estates in the South as a real aristocrat".[29] If there were corruption and crudities in the South also, or even democratic ideas, they were invisible to the cordial gaze of England. Sir John Acton, whose eyes were sharp to spy any menace to freedom, wrote after the war to General Lee: "I saw in State Rights the only availing check upon the absolutism of the sovereign will, and secession filled me with hope... I believed that the example of that great Reform [embodied

---

★ In some instances, for what they thought it was. The reader is reminded that I am not attempting here to say what the South (or the North) in fact was— aristocratic or democratic, or both (i.e., aristocratic in the Tidewater & other plantation areas, democratic in the mountains & western areas). This is a study of what Englishmen *thought* the South (& the North) was, which to a large degree was in accordance with the picture of the South given by such Southerners as Mason & Maury. The actuality of the Confederate South I must leave to be disputed by the many able historians who are concerned with it.

in the Confederate Constitution] would have blessed all the races
of mankind by establishing true freedom purged of the native
dangers and disorders of Republics. Therefore I deemed that you
were fighting the battles of our liberty, our progress, and our
civilization".[30] There was every reason for educated England to extend its sympathy to the politically and socially akin Confederacy;
England was perfectly true to what it had always been when it said:
"We heartily wish them God speed."[31]

An appreciation of Southern virtues was not, though, a prere-
quisite to wishing the Confederate States well. It was only necessary
to observe that Southern sabres were tearing and discrediting the
mantle of democracy that had fallen upon the battered shoulders
of the North. The first impulse of Englishmen who thought reform
had gone quite far enough was to rejoice: democracy on its own
native soil had failed; the 'republican bubble had burst'. Now at
last it was quite clear that universal suffrage made for instability
in government, and who—except the capful of 'Model
Republicans'—would be so mad as to risk such dangers in England?
"The democracy of America has been as great a failure as the
democracy of France,"[32] men wrote, and believed; and even "many
professing Radicals found their faith in democracy oozing out,
because universal suffrage had not prevented civil war."[33] A few
of the Radicals, notably John Bright (unlike Richard Cobden), held
to their faith in democracy and even went so far as to assert that
the North would win. Almost all England know they were wrong:
history which had foretold the disintegration foretold also the futility
of fire and sword to force back a people determined to be free. There
was one area of tacit agreement between the two groups in England:
a return to the pre-war position of two views as to the strength and
enduring qualities of democracy was impossible. Democracy would
be utterly discredited. Or, it would achieve an incredible triumph.

Gentlemen v. Cads

The principal distinction between the North and the South was that between democracy and aristocracy; but there had to be a reason for so fundamental a difference between nations which were, after all, both of English descent. Englishmen (and Southerners) discovered their reason in the varied origins of the original Thirteen Colonies: New England which was to dominate the North had been settled by discontented Puritans; Carolina and Virginia by gentlemen and Cavaliers. Perhaps Englishmen looked again at Thackeray's account of Castlewood in the Northern Neck of Virginia. [34] Then, if doubts remained as to whether Virginia remained the same in the 1860's, assurances from both Southerners and English travellers, with references to the Lees of Stratford Hall and other first families, were not wanting: "we must accept this much as fact, that it will take a good many generations yet to come to strip the Southern gentleman of that nobility which he inherits from the English Cavalier".[35] In the Northern background was the "narrow, fanatical, and originally sincere puritanism of their ancestors", but "the Virginians, Carolinians, and Georgians were...almost exclusively offshoots from the grand territorial stock of ancient English gentry—a noble caste...which has in nowise degenerated in either sex on the soil of the South".[36] The idea took deep root and lasted long past the war. Disraeli's Colonel Campian "was a gentleman of the South and with nothing puritanical about him."[37] An English traveller, wandering the Virginian battlefields in 1867, reflects upon what he considers the first cause of the war: "On one side of a faint and failing line...a race of Cavaliers...brave and haughty...[with] the graces which come of birth, of culture, of command...On the other side of that line...men of Puritan descent; shrewd merchants, skilful artisans...Which was to give the law...?"[38]

All this was reason enough to explain the difference between North and South, but a second plausible reason was discovered in the fact that, while the South remained unchanged and English,

Northern blood (and Northern ideas) had been adulterated by immigration from every corner of Europe, and the Northerners had
become an unEnglish race which could neither be liked nor trusted.
The M.P., Arthur Roebuck, said to a cheering crowd: "The North
will never be our friends. Of the South you can make friends. They
are Englishmen. They are not the scum and refuse of Europe."[39]
Expressed with more of feeling than tact, it was yet the judgement
of many because (like the Cavalier-Puritan theory) it had a degree
of demonstrable truth.★ Louis Blanc, a Union supporter whose
French blood ensured neutrality on the racial question wrote on
one occasion of "the not unfounded opinion that the North. . .has
lost much of its English origin, and that the true representatives
of the Saxon race in America are the Southerners". On another
occasion, more significantly, he observed that the whole war to the
English was "nothing else than a struggle between the English
aristocracy and the Irish or German plebeians. In the men of the
South they love and admire. . .their own race; in the men of the
North they detest what they regard as a confused mixture of
foreigners. For them, the 'gentlemen' are in one camp, and the 'cads'
in the other."[40] If a large proportion of the English upper and middle
classes, the gentlemen and those who aspired to be gentlemen, believed this—that the war resolved down to Gentlemen *versus* Cads,
foreign cads and English gentlemen—there can be small wonder that
England was 'Southern' or that the quality of its support was very
like patriotism. The idea of the South's being the English side was
strengthened by continual reports of large-scale Northern recruiting
in Ireland and in Europe; and also by numerous accounts of how
Southerners not only valued English friendship but "felt that the
English were of nearer kin to them than their Yankee brethren."[41]

★ Nowhere did I encounter from the supporters of the North what might be thought
the obvious answer, that it required such a mixture of 'immigrants' as Iberians,
Celts, Romans, Anglo-Saxons, Danes, Normans, with later infusions of French,
Flemish, & Dutch, in order to arrive at the pure English blood.

One writer quoted his friend, the great South Carolinian Calhoun, as saying: "We certainly feel ourselves English—how can we feel otherwise? Are we not entirely English?...Certainly all our sympathies are with England and with Englishmen".[42]

Thus the South's maintaining 'old English Constitutional government' and the North's debasing theirs with corruption and despotism could be, and were, explained by these differences of origin and blood. The explanation, indeed, made the whole war understandable: "It is this fact—that the Southerners are another people, and the natural desire which it creates to have an existence and a Government of their own—that is the chief cause of this convulsion."[43] This Anglo-Southern thesis also explained what at the same time proved the thesis: the sharp contrast, perceived with increasing passion, between the customs and manners of the two warring peoples. The Englishmen that favoured the South as the side of the English gentlemen began to fall in love with the Southerner: "You know he is a gentleman," said Disraeli's Duke; "he is not a Yankee. People make the greatest mistakes about these things. He is a gentleman of the South."[44] But if their affection for the Southerner deepened, so too did their loathing for the Northerner: and both of these sentiments were based on the events of the war. It was not, they were quite certain, a slavery war. It was a war between two different races: on the one side were the mongrel, alien Yankees, waging war with the harshness if not the boldness of the Ironsides; on the other, gallant English gentlemen with the gay courage, colour, and courtesy of the Cavaliers.*

Could any such view honestly be held by a literate Englishman? The answer is, that such a view *was* held with unmistakable sincerity by intelligent, educated Englishmen, and by Southerners as well.

---

* If this is thought to be extreme, one may compare it with neutral views in other wars—for instance, England's view of the Greeks & their oppressors early in the century, or America's view of the English & the 'Huns' in 1916, or in 1940.

We have considered the thesis of origins—Cavalier gentlemen as opposed to Puritans-plus-European-immigrants—which explained the differences of North and South; but, also, the observed differences confirmed the thesis. If we are to understand how Englishmen could quite honestly hold the belief that the war was one of 'Gentlemen' v. 'Cads', we must examine in some detail how certain events appeared to them.

The Northerners, then, were 'cads' because—to use a recurring phrase—of 'Butler, brag, and beastliness'. As to 'brag', it may be said as fact that there were Northern politicians and newspapers that were not committed to understatement. Southern newspapers seldom came through the blockade, and such militant Southern boasts as that one Southerner was the equal of ten Yankees were unpublicized. ★ But the air was filled with Northern assurances of what their armies were about to do to the 'Rebels'. And their armies lost the battles. "It is right to remember", wrote one friend of the Union, "that the North...has been far from displaying the qualities likely to be appreciated in this country: I mean the external dignity of attitude,...a countenance stern and haughty, a quiet air, absence of ostentation and brag. In England...people are more inclined to advocate a bad cause defended in proper form than a good cause badly defended. ...[And they have] observed that the government of Jefferson Davis spoke little and hit hard, came forth calm in adversity and modest in success, kept its eye fixed on its purpose, and strode towards it with resolute step".[45] So wrote one whose sympathies were Northern. Another Union sympathizer viewed with alarm this contrast in the impressions made by the warring Americas; he feared that England was being "carried away by...the superior pluck, the unanimity, the energy, the military talent, and the modest but earnest proclamations of the South—[whilst being repelled] by the mismanagement, the divided counsels,

★ Today the more candid Southerners admit that it was only five.

the boastful language, the political corruption of the North".[46] Englishmen wrote mockingly of the bombast that always preceded the advance of the huge Union armies which, by their own accounts, were somehow always outnumbered on the field of battle. More seriously, they wrote that the "Southern Confederacy stands on infinitely higher ground, and their conduct gives them undeniable claims to our approval and respect. They have been moderate, reserved, self-reliant, indomitably firm."[47]

Brag and bravado, as it seemed to the English, could not endear the United States to them, but such things had an amusing side. Not so the 'beastliness', by which was meant a certain vindictiveness of spirit and deed. One should remember that this was an age when Englishmen hoped, and on Darwinian grounds believed, that war would grow more civilized and decent until it quite disappeared. Thus they were genuinely shocked at the 'total-war' tactics of some of the ablest Union generals (such as Sherman), and also by what seemed an unrealistic and unfair refusal by the United States to regard the Confederates as honourable opponents or, indeed, as anything other than wicked traitors. "We must go back to the era of the thirty years war, perhaps to the days of Attila," wrote an Englishman in 1866, "before we can find anything parallel to the ruthless spirit in which this war has been waged by a people, who claim to be guides to the rest of mankind in a path of civilization....Even the severities of Blucher and his Prussians...were tender mercies compared to the atrocities of Sherman, Sheridan, and Grant, practiced on their unfortunate brethren of the South...the total devastation of every region where a Northern army sets its foot...were the war measures of the North."[48] Englishmen had never heard of 'total war', but they totally condemned their first sight of it. The Evangelical leader, the Earl of Shaftesbury, wrote to the Confederate Commissioner in London:—

The recent news from America contains an order from General Pope [U.S.A.] for the devastation of the Virginia Valley, and for the total disregard, by his troops, of all the rights of private property. It contains, moreover, the details of a public meeting, held at Washington, where President Lincoln...took the chair, and which, under his sanction, passed...the following resolutions:...'Let the Union be preserved, or the country be made a desert. We are convinced that the leaders of the rebellion will never return to their allegiance, and, therefore, they shall be regarded and treated as irreclaimable traitors, who are to be stripped of all their possessions, deprived of their lives, or expelled from the country.'...I was, I confess, taken aback by such an expression of deliberate ferocity from the lips of a civilized and Christian people....I am certain that the first sentiment of the bulk of my countrymen...will be a prayer to God that the Confederate States may not be tempted to enter upon reprisals, and that the war...may be conducted, on one side, at least, according to those military rules which humanity has suggested and observed for the mitigation of this fearful scourge...

Later the noble Earl wrote again:—

I am deeply thankful to read...that the Confederate Provost Marshall has issued an order the very reverse of General Pope's...This is Christianlike and politic...[49]

The contrast between North and South was impossible to overlook. When the Confederate army followed General Lee into the North, the troops were well-behaved and the local authorities were paid for supplies and "assured of good treatment for themselves and their properties...according to the Southern policy".[50] Later, when the Northerners were boasting that a bird must carry its own rations to fly over the once-lush Valley of Virginia, when Atlanta and Columbia were in flames, Englishmen remembered the Southern restraint. Evangelical Christians who retained a hope that, despite President Lincoln's denial, the North might be fighting to free the slaves were faced with something of a moral dilemma: whether to condemn the United States for their methods of warfare or to support them as the better choice to end slavery. In simple fact, the South, caught up in a dream of chivalry, attempted to make war according to a gentlemanly eighteenth-century code that was already old-fashioned; and the North was, with regard to the actual development of warfare, very advanced. ★

But the North won few battles until late in the war and, consequently, the more ruthless tactics were not at first displayed. What *was* displayed—which brings us to the 'Butler' of the summary 'Butler, brag and beastliness'—were the personal actions of certain United States leaders, in particular, General Benjamin F. Butler of Massachusetts, who became to thousands of Englishmen the type of the 'Yankee'. Butler was not, in fact, one of the principal Federal commanders in the field, but he must occupy a principal place in this study, for he—not Grant or Sherman—became the most famous, or infamous, of the United States military men. Butler's was the name that was contrasted with the name of Lee. Partly this was owing to the fact that the earlier Union commanders—coming to the command, losing a battle, and being replaced—were seldom long in the public eye. Butler, however, won an enduring notoriety in a day. He had been appointed to his rank for political reasons by Lincoln and had actually little or no military experience; he was given command of the troops occupying captured New Orleans. There he issued the Order that made him the most infamous figure of a Major General in the English-speaking world. The Order stated that if any of the—

> women calling themselves 'ladies of New Orleans'. . . shall by word, gesture, or movement, insult or show contempt for any officer or soldier of the United States, she shall be regarded

★ A.J. Toynbee in *A Study of History* (v IV, p 142) remarks: "War had become a more terrible thing by the year 1865. . . than it had been in 1861".

and held liable to be treated as a woman of the town plying her avocation.

A growl of anger shuddered through all England. The Prime Minister, Lord Palmerston, protested this 'revolting outrage' to the United States Minister. The Order, wrote an English lady, "ought to arouse all the indignation of woman; and all the avenging Chivalry of man...throughout the whole civilized world."[51] The press devoted leaders to the 'crime against humanity'. Pamphlets portrayed a Butler "who boasted that he would conquer the South by 'the light of the smoking and rebellious cities,'"[52] who "plundered the inhabitants...[and] tortured a poor helpless female until she died a raving maniac, for laughing at the misfortunes of his soldiers",[53] and who "issued a proclamation containing a more coarse and licentious insult to the ladies of a Southern city than was possibly ever printed before..."[54] Butler became 'Beast Butler' in England as well as the South, and the type not only of the Northern military man but of the New England Yankee. The incident has an importance beyond the infamy of Butler: A large number of Englishmen now became firmly convinced—especially in the absence of any disavowal of Butler by Lincoln—that the United States, unable to win battles, were waging war on women. This idea, perhaps, could not seriously have been held, as it was in fact held, were it not for the reality of Butler's Order. A long letter, published in London, from an anonymous Southern lady described the burning of her home by the Yankees, and pictured the slave cabin where she and her little children had now to find shelter; the war, she said, had originally been caused by dislike but *"Now we hate each other, and can never reunite."*[55] A Maryland lady, in a Federal prison, wrote for English readers:— "That time—when I, in common with all our people, looked up with pride and veneration to the...stars and stripes—appears...with the years before the Flood. I look back...through a haze of blood and horror."[56] Thackeray spoke with a trembling voice of the South Carolinian lady whom he had loved and who had died alone, her mother and sister refused permission by the Northerners to go to her side; Thackeray in fact (Henry Adams wrote) "never doubted that the Federals made a business of harrowing the tenderest feelings of women...in order to punish their opponents."[57] If so distinguished a writer and observer, and one who had travelled in America, believed this, there can be little wonder that with many Englishmen it became a horrified conviction that the Northerners made war on women and the helpless. They had what they considered to be quite adequate proof in a series of events stretching from Butler's 'invitation to outrage' to the Northern clergyman who was reported to have urged the complete extermination of Southern whites—men, women and children.[58]

The elements, then, of 'Butler, Brag, and Beastliness' meant, respectively: war on women and the helpless; loud threats unmatched by performance; and a peculiarly savage vindictiveness. A single event was the crown and culmination of all three—Lincoln's Emancipation Proclamation. Since this document now, nearly a century after Lincoln's 'martyrdom' in the hour of victory, is quite commonly regarded as the noblest monument in the life of a great humanitarian, it is a little difficult to see how it could be regarded then as the ultimate atrocity. To do so, one must lay aside one's awareness of the eventual emancipation of the slaves and consider the Proclamation in January of 1863, when it was issued. Then the Confederate States were winning the war. Only a few days before, Lee had smashed Burnside at Fredericksburg. The Proclamation freed all the slaves *within* the Confederate lines, that is, the slaves which the Federal armies were manifestly unable to reach. These slaves were grouped on the isolated plantations, controlled for the most part by the women since their gentlemen were off to the wars. The only possible effect of the Proclamation would be the dreaded servile insurrection (that which John Brown was hanged for inciting). *Either a slave rising—or nothing.* So Englishmen saw it. Lincoln's insincerity was regarded as proven by two things: his earlier denial of any lawful right or wish to free the slaves; and, especially, his *not* freeing the slaves in 'loyal' Kentucky and other United States areas or even in Confederate areas occupied by United States troops, such as New Orleans. It should be remembered that the horrors of the Indian Mutiny, as well as a slave uprising in St Domingo, were in every memory. We shall consider emancipation again in another light: here we are concerned only to see it as it was seen by those horrified Englishmen—and they were many—who could see it only as a last frightfulness. 'Lincoln's last card' it was called by the leader-writers. It is no exaggeration to say that the reserved, and then executed, threat of sudden emancipation was looked upon in much the same way as we looked upon the reserved menace of poison gas in the late war with Nazi Germany. Emancipation of the enemy's slaves, if it were anything at all, would be a horror. The slaves, of course, did not rise—hence, 'brag'—but *had* they risen (and it is difficult to see how anyone, including President Lincoln, could have been sure they would not rise), the Englishmen who held the Proclamation to be intended to incite an uprising would have got a grim justification. Even after the war, there were still Englishmen who believed that the Proclamation was, "on the score of morality, the greatest public crime of modern times.... It would be well for the authors...if the miscarriage of its purpose could wipe away its heavy guiltiness."[59]

When Englishmen, some of whom might otherwise have supported the United States, turned away from 'Butler, brag, and beastliness' to the slave-holding Confederate States, they saw the Southern men who did more to win English sympathy than all the logic of State Rights and free trade. Around the remote splendour of Lee after the Seven Days, were the other officers of the Army of Northern Virginia who captured the imagination of England, particularly Stuart, the Rupert of the Confederate cavalry, and Stonewall Jackson—whose "pure patriotic valour and self-abnegation", in the words of a widely-read military historian, would be long-remembered "in the history of the country he helped to create."[60] And when this same author, Captain Chesney of Sandhurst, writes of Lee—even in the Gettysburg defeat—no words could be more admiring: As Lee turned "back to their duty all who could bear a weapon, whilst using (as has ever been his wont) rather the tenderness of a parent than the sternness of a general...the wounded stopped to cheer their beloved chief; and the groups of loiterers seeking the rear for some trifling hurt, turned back to seek their forsaken colours, and to stand or die with 'Uncle Robert.'...all who looked on him recognized the calm serenity of a hero equal to the crisis of the hour."[61] The normal, thoughtful Englishman, who read his *Times* or *Guardian,* and perhaps his Chesney, found that, regardless of his position on slavery, he could not help sympathizing with a cause represented by such men as these—and perhaps, quite humanly, he concluded that the cause supported by such men *must* be a just one. Even if the moral issue in the war had been as clear as it is now commonly supposed to have been, many Englishmen would still have judged both sides by the men and deeds that represented them. And the South could hardly have been better armed for such judgement by England. "I have a sort of idea that the Virginian character is realized in Lee", wrote the Marquess of Lothian: "Suffice it to say, that the 'Old Dominion' has produced the general who stands second to Wellington among the great soldiers of English blood in the present century...If all the stories about cruelty to negroes were as true as most of them are false—...even then the Confederacy might claim to stand on a pretty high level on the strength of having produced...Lee, Stuart, and Jackson. All of them have been distinguished, not more for their courage, their genius..., and the enthusiasm which they have been able to excite in their soldiers, than for the gentle and unselfish character which has been common to all; and for all of them, and for others who, if less celebrated, are on every ground worthy to be ranked beside them, the Confederacy is indebted to the single

State of Virginia.''[62]★

One thing only remains to be said on the subject of 'Gentlemen v. Cads' if, indeed, it is not implicit in the foregoing pages: The sympathy, the liking, the enthusiasm for the South were genuine; they were positive things, not—as has so often been suggested— mere anti-Northernism. There were first-thoughts, to be sure, about free trade and the discrediting of democracy; but then England discovered that she had come to like these valiant 'English gentlemen of the South' very much. The crew of an English man-of-war, lying in Hampton Roads, watching the small CSS *Jamestown* go in under the guns of the Federal fortress and capture a prize, were "unable to restrain their generous impulses, [and] from the captain to the side-boy, cheered [her] to the very echo.''[63] Thus, in a passable parallel, England herself swung at anchor and, watching the small brave South engage the formidable fortress of the United States, could not forbear to cheer. This English response is "something more than an interested calculation, there is a passionate, unthinking infatuation, and...a real tenderness of heart.''[64] General Lee alone proved that the Southerners were 'English gentlemen', and 'Butler, brag, and beastliness' that the Northerners were 'cads.' English gentlemen could have but one choice, with few exceptions. Long after the cause of the gentlemen had gone down into irrevocable defeat, Sir Alexander Cockburn wrote:

> Whatever the cause in which they are exhibited, devotion and courage will ever find respect, and they did so in this instance. Men could not see in the united people of these vast provinces, thus risking all in the cause of nationality and independence, the common case of rebels disturbing peace and order on ac-

★ In 1914 the First Lord of the Admiralty, writing on war matters to the Prime Minister, said with reference to the Forces: "It has been stated that 50,000 or 60,000 Americans have volunteered, including a number of Virginians...." — W.S. Churchill, *The World Crisis 1911-1914,* London, 1923, p 272 (Letter quoted in full but no more on Virginians).

count of imaginary grievances... They gave credit to the statesmen and warriors of the South...for the higher motives which ennoble political action, and all the opprobrious terms which might be heaped upon the cause in which he fell could not persuade the world that the earth beneath which Stonewall Jackson rests does not cover the remains of a patriot and a hero...[65]

The Cause of Freedom

The 'cause of nationality and independence'—that, at least, was clear to the English observers beyond the sea. The origins of the war might be in doubt, but the indisputable fact was that the Southerners were fighting, with fortitude and resolution, for freedom. They asked only independence which the North only denied. To a good many thoughtful Englishmen, Abraham Lincoln, in reasserting a repudiated Government and a rejected brotherhood by the bayonet, was but walking in the grassless way of the despots of Austria and Russia.

The North and the South, in Lord John Russell's famous phrase, were contending, on the one side for empire, on the other for independence. The words struck the imagination of England with the ring of truth. That the United States, which once had fought for independence, should now be fighting for empire might be an irony but not a surprise. The acquisition of the vast Louisiana territory and Texas, the ruthless dispossession of the Red Indians, the talk of 'Manifest Destiny', the threatening gestures towards Canada—all looked like empire, and rather an aggressive one. "We were tired of hearing continually of the intended annexation of Canada, and of the kind sufferance by which we ourselves were permitted to exist."[66] To an England for the moment interested not in empire but in trade and progress, the United States were a threat to the peace of the world. Thus, like Lord Palmerston, many Englishmen

who were not especially afraid of democracy desired from the first
the independence of the Confederacy "as a diminution of a
dangerous power".[67] Since Seward, the United States Secretary of
State, was even then urging upon his colleagues his 'foreign war
panacea'—a plan to attempt the reunion of the states by a war upon
England—the term 'dangerous power' is not without justice. In the
House of Commons, Roebuck expressed his hope that the "great
bully of the world" would be permanently split:[68] such sentiments
towards a nation with which England was at peace were not often
expressed in Parliament; perhaps the remarkable thing is that they
were expressed at all. There can be no doubt, indeed, that many
Englishmen were conscious of relief at the end of what they felt
to be an aggressive and 'overgrown' power: "And who, let it be freely
asked and truly answered, in the whole of this great community
of the United Kingdom, except some...obstinate fanatics, is not
rejoiced at the breaking up of that monstrous...United States?"[69]

It was clear enough that the United States had engaged in empire-
building in the recent past—though few Englishmen appreciated how
much of this was owing to Southern expansionists and 'Warhawks'.
Because the diminished United States were both aggressive and
hostile to England (and nearer to Canada), they got the blame. But,
whatever the aggressiveness past and present, the great question now
was, whether their attempt to conquer the seceded states was a just
exercise of sovereignty or was an imperialistic conquest for the sake
of domination. Unlike European revolutions, the Southern secession involved an appeal both to constitutional rights and to natural
rights. Since the Englishmen we are concerned with—'the educated
million'—were able to, and in many cases did, form an opinion on
these appeals, we should attempt to see how, in the 1860's, the
reasoning went.

With regard to the constitutional appeal, the Southern states
asserted—as in fact most of the Northern states had done at one
time or another in the past—that sovereign states had, in the con-

stitutional compact, delegated certain *limited* powers to a federal government; and that they could at will resume those powers—in short, secede from a purely voluntary association of states, in effect, a 'United Nations'. The Northern states, under the influence of a growing 'Americanism', asserted, with hesitation at first, that they could not. The Southern states further asserted that, even if they could not legally secede, no power had been delegated to the Federal Government (had actually been rejected when proposed at the Constitutional Convention) which would enable it to coerce a seceded state back into the Union. The Northern states, nevertheless, and not without many objectors, exercised such power—maintaining, eventually, that the *states* had not seceded (a sort of legal fiction) but only conspirators *in* the states. England, not so many years distant from John Locke, was impressed with the Southern legal case. And not, noticeably, with the Northern. James Spence's *The American Union*—much the most popular book of the war—contained "An Inquiry into Secession as a Constitutional Right". Its careful and lucid argument, which must have shaped the opinions of many of its readers, concluded: "that secession is a just and clear constitutional right of the States, and no violation of...the Federal compact."[70] In a speech, later, this same Englishman stressed the fact "that this power of coercion...[is] utterly opposed to the principle of the compact, which was that of free-will.—(Cheers.) Hence...[it] has not only no warrant in the Constitution, but is the wrongful exercise of a power which was deliberately excluded from it."[71] Quite apart from the contrary assertions of the two nations, there were certain events which pointed the way towards a decision on this matter. Coercion was obviously more dangerous and delicate ground for the North than the simple denial of the disputable right of secession. Thus when Virginia and the upper South withdrew only in protest against being party to the coercion of the Deep South, the action had a powerful effect on English thought. So, too, had the arbitrary and illegal actions of the Lincoln administration in suspending the writ of *habeas cor-*

pus, shutting down newspapers, imprisoning men without trial, and placing Maryland under martial law; the urgency of the danger that persuaded the Government to do these things was not nearly so apparent in England as the conclusion that a Government which showed so little respect for the law in connexion with basic rights was capable of—and probably was—bending the law to its own purposes in denying secession by force. Similarly, emancipation—clearly and admittedly illegal—confirmed many thoughtful Englishmen in the belief that the whole United States position was illegal and invalid. But perhaps the strongest of these arguments from the Constitution, an argument stated by every pro-Southern writer, was the one derived from the North's action in forming a new state out of part of western Virginia, for the Constitution (Art. IV:3) unmistakably prohibited precisely that. Thus the United States position as the upholder of the Constitution seemed fatally undermined. Englishmen might support the Union on other grounds, but not on legal; and those whose inclinations led them to consider issues from the point of view of the law tended to take the Confederate side. The answer, then, to the question, whether on Constitutional grounds the United States were justly exercising sovereign power or unjustly indulging in conquest, was for most Englishmen who thought about it:—"I believe...the right of secession is so clear, that if the South had wished to do so for no better reason than that it could not bear to be beaten in an election, like a sulky schoolboy out of temper at not winning a game, and had submitted the question to the decision of any court of law in Europe, she would have carried her point."[72]

In books and pamphlets and articles, in speeches and doubtless in conversation, Englishmen discussed all the Constitutional questions that were equally discussed in the South: whether secession was or was not legal, whether the authority to coerce a state was implicit or withheld, whether ultimate sovereignty reposed in the people of a state or in the whole people of the United States, whether minorities had rights that could stand against an opposing majority. This last question was on a somewhat deeper level than those of strict Constitutional interpretation. As Locke and the Revolutionary founders had defined it, freedom was a state of society existing under a constitution that protected the rights of the minority, whether only a handful of people or millions. But the Northerners were asserting the right of a majority of the people—there being, now, a majority in the North—to deny the constitutional rights of the minority (in the particular point at issue, the right to take their slave property where they would). The South said, with some truth, that they were taking their stand on the Constitution as its drawers intended it to be; and that the North was attacking the most fundamental principle of a constitution by holding that it could not protect a minority if the majority willed otherwise. The Englishman whose political philosophy stemmed from Locke was inclined to stand with the South.

But there were higher grounds—the fundamental or natural rights of revolution and freedom—where most Englishmen preferred to stand. How did the Southern case look to them from there? Since 1688 the liberal mind in Europe had made into a fundamental article of political faith the doctrine, which found expression in the Declaration of Independence, that just government is based upon the consent of the governed. If there was one clear truth in connexion with the war between the American states, it was that the South did *not* consent to be governed by the United States Government. The North's early assertion that the rebellion was being made by a few conspirators in each Southern state was no longer credible in England after the first battle. Therefore, in attempting to reimpose its authority by force, the United States Government, for those who held the doctrine simply, was unjust. Slavery did not enter in since the slaves were not revolting—not, that is, withholding consent. The North maintained that consent was that of the 'whole people' of the former Union, of whom they were a majority; this did not carry conviction in an England that was preparing to give her colonies freedom upon demand. Indeed, the Northern interpretation of consent could be used to justify any reconquest—including the English reconquest of the Thirteen. The war remained, therefore, for most Liberals an unjust one on the part of the United States, which were seen as beyond question deserting their ancient principles. "In no country in the world were allegiance and the rights of rulers so generally despised," wrote one Englishman with bitter mockery; "in no country were 'rebels' so honoured and the memory of rebels so esteemed....Then can we believe what is now said,...that ten million Americans wished to set up an independent Government, and that thereupon they have been sabred and shot down for exercising the very right consecrated...in 1776;...that the word 'rebel' is a term of reproach in Boston itself, the very cradle of rebellion...?"[73] A cool scholar in 95 pages of dispassionate legal analysis displayed but one hint of feeling, when he said scornfully that the Northerner, "who has ever piqued himself on sympathizing with revolt all over the world,...now knows not how to pardon the faintest symptom of an inclination...to give a fair hearing to the South;...he whose first axiom has been that no Government could be just which was not founded on consent, now clings with all the tenacity of the veriest despot to the forcible maintenance of a sovereignty against which millions rebel."[74] Late in the war Earl Russell said in the House of Lords: "It is dreadful to think that hundreds of thousands of men are being slaughtered for the purpose of preventing the Southern States from acting on those very principles of independence which, in 1776, were asserted by the whole of America against this country."[75] For those Englishmen who held the principle of consent to be sacred, and very many of the most thoughtful and intelligent did so with the utmost sincerity, no talk of democracy or slavery could in anywise alter or conceal the unmistakable fact that the South did not consent.

Besides constitutional rights and the right of consent, there was still a third right—actually a variation of consent—which was appealed to: the right of nationalities to be free. To Englishmen the

South had proved itself a nationality in the most unequivocal way, regardless of origin and blood, by fighting for independence. Just so had the Thirteen Colonies, regardless of origin and blood, asserted their independence and nationhood. "I can well remember," wrote W.E.H. Lecky, "how the illustrious historian, Mr. Grote,...who...always formed his opinions with an austere independence and integrity, was accustomed to speak on the subject... He could not, he said, understand how those who had been so lately preaching in the most unqualified terms that all large bodies of men had an absolute, unimpeachable, indefeasible right to choose for themselves their form of government, and that the growing recognition of this right was one of the first conditions of progress and liberty, could support or applaud the Federal Government in imposing on the Southern States a government which they detested, and in overriding by force their evident and unquestionable desire."[76] The struggle in Italy had very recently brought the doctrine of the right of nationalities to the fore, and it was nowhere more enthusiastically accepted than in England. And if Englishmen sympathized passionately with Italy,—"how then could they consistently withhold their sympathies from the South, while struggling for national independence, with a heroism not surpassed by anything recorded in history"?[77] The Confederates, there seemed no possible doubt, were but one more instance of an oppressed nationality fighting for freedom. That the United States were capable of oppression was regarded as proved by their harsh and arbitrary actions in Maryland and elsewhere. The argument-by-analogy (that is, the Southerners and the Italians) was strengthened still more by the circumstances of the Poles waging their hopeless war against Russia at the same time as the Southerners were struggling against the United States. Englishmen now recalled that when *they* were fighting against the overwhelming power of the despot, Napoleon, the United States joined in the war—against England. They also remembered, and pointed out to their countrymen, the ostentatious friendship with Russia that the United States displayed during the

Crimean war. The spectacle of two giant powers, on the friendliest
of terms with each other, both suppressing with what seemed to
be exceptional savagery bravely fighting revolutionaries, was sug-
gestive to a degree that few Englishmen could miss, or were allowed
to miss. And when (again, as it *seemed*) the oppressed nationality,
in the one case, was an English nationality, when the valiant revolutionaries were English gentlemen fighting against alien armies and
despotic power,—there can be small wonder that a flame of sympathy for the South burned in England.

Thus for the greater number of thoughtful Englishmen, whether
they took their stand on the right by law, the right of minorities,
the right of the governed to withhold consent, or the right of nationalities to be free, it was clear that the United States were not
exercising a just sovereignty but were engaged in conquest for the
sake of dominion. "Had the secession put in peril the power of the
North to protect itself against external force, . . . the war might have
been justifiable; but. . . [it] endangered nothing but the prideful
dream of a prodigious supremacy, a gigantic national power".[78]
But that dream could never come true, the United States could never
conquer the South. The books of Southerners published in London were unanimous in the determination never to submit to the
hated North:—"Those men whom I once called friends. . . have. . .
hounded on host after host of greedy invaders. . . upon the beloved
valleys. . . Many who were dear to me have been slain, fighting in
defense of all that makes life of value. Instead of friends, I see. . .
only mortal enemies."[79] The passion of this woman of the South
found an answer in England: All the abstract arguments were lost
"in the great war-cry of the South—Independence!"[80]—"they only demand from their enemies the right to govern
themselves"[81]—"the cause of the South is the cause of freedom".[82]
Disraeli's Southern officer "was fighting for freedom all his life".[83]
The very word—*freedom!*—had a splendour in the sixties. Many
years later, W.E.H. Lecky wrote:—

The Southern States proclaimed the right of nationalities, demanded their independence, and proved their earnestnes and their unanimity by arguments that were far more unequivocal than any doubtful plebiscite. For four long years they defended their cause on the battle-field with heroic courage, against overwhelming odds, and at the sacrifice of everything that men most desire.... no one who looks carefully into the history of the American revolution, who observes the languor,... the frequent pusillanimity, the absence of all strong and unselfish enthusiasm... in great portions of the revolted colonies, and their entire dependence for success on foreign assistance, will doubt that the Southern States in the War of Secession exhibited an incomparably higher level of courage, tenacity, and self-sacrifice. No nation in the nineteenth century has maintained its nationhood with more courage and unanimity.[84]

This chapter has been designed to show not the extent but the nature of English sympathy for the Confederacy—so far as possible in the words of those who felt or observed it. There were, essentially, four great appeals: The first was the golden dream of progress and prosperity through free trade. The second and greater was the fear for constitutional liberties and for stability under democracy—the 'tyranny of the mob'. Still more important was the concept of kinship with the 'English gentlemen of the South' struggling against unEnglish 'cads'. And greatest of all was the cry of freedom. These were four streams that came together to create the flood of Southern sympathy, a flood so strong that a man who sympathized with the enemy of the South was actually called 'unEnglish'. The chapter must be ended with the words of two Englishmen, one a skilled doctor writing in 1863 to a Northerner, the other a great nobleman writing in 1864, who between them bring all the four streams together:—

[The Physician]
You will be solicitous to know the state of public feeling

here. . . I fear I can say little that is satisfactory. . . Events that
have occurred. . . have all tended to obliterate sympathy with
the northern cause, even among those who were most attached
to it at first. It may be well to mention. . . some of the causes. . .
I would name as such. . . the conduct of General Butler, and
some other local authorities, on the scene of war; the report
of the committee on fraudulent contracts by persons in high
office; the proofs variously given of the excitement of more
southern sentiment in the North than of Union feeling in the
South;. . . the arbitrary form the government has assumed in
the North; and your recent tariffs. . . I might name one or two
other causes which I perceive to have effect, namely, a certain
sympathy with the South as the weaker party, and an admiration of their unexpected vigour and unity of action, and the
dignified tone of such of their public documents as have
reached us; and further, the intimation we get. . . of the still-
continued violence of feeling in the North against England,—a
feeling which is regarded here as fully unwarranted by anything
that has occurred. . .

                                —Sir Henry Holland, 1863[85]

[The Nobleman]
This conflict has been signalised by the exhibition of some of
the best and some of the worst qualities that war has ever
brought out. It has produced. . . a contempt of principles; . . . a
deep and widely-extended corruption. . . the public faith scan-
dalously violated both towards friends and enemies; the liberty of the citizen at the mercy of arbitrary power;. . . the most
brutal inhumanity in the conduct of the war itself. . . all the
old horrors of barbarous warfare, which Europe is beginning
to be ashamed of, and new refinements of cruelty thereto added
by way of illustrating the advance of the age of knowledge.
It has also produced qualities and phenomena the opposite of
these; an ardour and devotedness of patriotism which might
alone be enough to make us proud of the century to which we
belong;. . . a stainless good faith under extremely difficult cir-

cumstances;...a heroism in the field...which can match anything that history has to show;...a most scrupulous regard for the rights of hostile property... It is true that it can hardly be said that the Federal atrocities are unprecedented...[but] I am not going a hair's-breadth beyond what I soberly and sincerely believe, in saying that the Confederates have, in almost every respect, surpassed anything that has ever been known. [It is the] most splendid instance of a nation's defense of its liberties that the world has seen...

—The Marquess of Lothian, 1864.[86]

[1] A.J. B. Beresford Hope, *A Popular View of the American Civil War,* London, 1861 (and later editions), p 16. [Hereafter: Hope, *View*]

[2] A.J.B. Beresford Hope, *England, the North & the South,* London, 1862 (2nd edit.), p 39. [Hereafter: Hope, *England*]

[3] James Spence, *Southern Independence: An Address, &c.,* London & Glasgow, 1863, p 17. [Hereafter: Spence, *Independence*]

[4] Mason, p 253.

[5] Quoted by Goldwin Smith, *Letter on Southern Independence: a Letter to a Whig Member of the Southern Independence Association,* London, 1864, p 34.

[6] Owsley, pp 572-574.

[7] Louis Blanc, v II, p 99, quoting Lord Vane Tempest.

[8] Hope, *England,* p 35.

[9] A.J.B. Beresford Hope, *The Social & Political Bearings of the American Disruption,* London, 1863, pp 40-41. [Hereafter: Hope, *Bearings*]

[10] *Hansard's Parliamentary Debates,* 3rd Series, London, 1862, v CLXV, 1158-1230. [Hereafter: *Hansard*]

[11] J.W. Cowell, *Southern Secession: a Letter Addressed to Captain M.T. Maury, Confederate Navy, &c,* London, 1862, pp 40-42. [Hereafter: Cowell, *Secession*]

[12] *Ibid,* p 65

[13] Matthew Arnold, *Mixed Essays,* London, 1879, p 23.

[14] Henry Pelling, *op.cit.,* p 4, quoting G.S. Venables, leader-writer of *The Times.* Also quoted, with variations, by Jordan & Pratt, p 68.

[15] Alexis de Tocqueville, *Democracy in America,* (1st published 1835 & 1840), Oxford, 1946, p 268 & pp 279-280. [Hereafter: De Tocqueville]

[16] *The Times, (History),* p 373.

[17] C.B. Adderly, *Letter. . . on the Present Relations of England with the Colonies,* London, 1862, p vi.

[18] E.W. Field & C.G. Loring, *Correspondence on the Present Relations Between Great Britain & the United States of America,* Boston, 1862, p 28.

[19] Hope, *View,* p 10.

[20] Mrs H. Grote, *The Personal Life of George Grote,* London, 1873, p 262, quoting a letter of George Grote. [Hereafter: Grote]

[21] T.C. Gratten, *England & the Disrupted States of America,* London, 1861, p 14. [Hereafter: Grattan]

[22] Hope, *View,* p 8.

[23] Spence, *Independence,* p 38.

[24] Hope, *England,* p 3.

[25] James Spence, *The American Union, its Effect on National Character & Policy, &c.,* London, 1862, p 60. [Hereafter: Spence, *Union*]

[26] Grote, p 314.

[27] Hope, *England,* p 34.

[28] Hope, *View,* p 10.
[29] Benjamin Disraeli, *Lothair,* (first published 1870), 1927, p 195.
[30] D.S. Freeman, *R.E. Lee,* 4 vol., London & New York, 1935, v IV, pp 516-517. [Hereafter: Freeman, *Lee*]
[31] Charles Lempriere (St Johns, Oxford), *The American Crisis Considered,* London, 1861, p 224.
[32] C. Taylor, *The Probable Causes & Consequences of the American War,* Liverpool & London, 1864, p 30. [Hereafter: C. Taylor, *Causes*]
[33] John Watts, *The Facts of the Cotton Famine,* Manchester, 1866, p 105.
[34] See above, pp 26-27.
[35] A Recent Tourist, *The Right of Recognition, a Sketch of the Present Policy of the Confederate States,* London, 1862, p 8. [Hereafter: Recent Tourist]
[36] J.W. Cowell, *France & the Confederate States,* London & Paris, 1865, p 9 & p 13.
[37] Disraeli, *Lothair,* pp 199-200.
[38] W.H. Dixon, *The New America,* 2 vol., London, 1867, v. II, pp 314-315.
[39] R.E. Leader, *Life & Letters of J.A. Roebuck,* London, 1897, p 296.
[40] Louis Blanc, v II, p 99 & p 209.
[41] W.H. Dixon, *op.cit.,* v II, p 319.
[42] Cowell, *Secession,* p 30.
[43] Spence, *Independence,* p 17.
[44] Disraeli, *Lothair,* pp 199-200.
[45] Louis Blanc, 2nd Ser., v I, p 121.
[46] W.E. Baxter, *The Social Condition of the Southern States of America,* London, 1862, pp 3-4.
[47] Grattan, p 14.
[48] Locke, pp 16-17.
[49] Mason, pp 308-309 (letters dated 19 August & 23 September 1862).
[50] Captain C.C. Chesney, *A Military View of Recent Campaigns in Virginia & Maryland,* 2 vol., London, 1863, v I, p 146.
[51] A Southern Lady, *The Woes of War: A Letter of Sorrow,* London, 1862, from the Preface by Englishwoman Pauline Vyver, pp 3-4 [Hereafter: A Southern Lady]
[52] Hope, *Bearings,* p 7.
[53] C. Taylor, *Causes,* pp 16-17.
[54] J.H. Stack, *Historic Doubts Relative to the American War,* Birmingham, 1862, p 15. [Hereafter: Stack, *Historic Doubts*]
[55] A Southern Lady, p 13.
[56] (Mrs) Rose Greenhow, *My Imprisonment & the First Year of Abolition Rule at Washington,* London, 1863, p 3.
[57] Henry Adams, *The Education of Henry Adams,* London, 1919, p 131.
[58] Nemo, *Remarks on the Policy of Recognizing the Independence of the Southern States of North America,* London, 1863, p 14.

[59] Locke, pp 12-13.
[60] Captain C.C. Chesney, *A Military View of Recent Campaigns in Virginia & Maryland,* 2 vol., London, 1863, v I, pp 229-230. [Hereafter: Chesney]
[61] Chesney, v II, p 94.
[62] LOTHIAN, p 157 & pp 164-166.
[63] Jefferson Davis, *The Rise & Fall of the Confederate Government,* 2 vol., London, 1881, v II, p 201.
[64] Louis Blanc, v II, p 209.
[65] Bulloch, v II, pp 313-314.
[66] J.H. Kennaway, *On Sherman's Track, or, The South After the War,* London, 1867, p 267. [Hereafter: Kennaway]
[67] J. Morley, *The Life of William Ewart Gladstone,* 3 vol., London, 1903, v II, p 82. (The phrase is Gladstone's; the sentiment Palmerston's)
[68] *Hansard,* CLXXI, 1771-80.
[69] Grattan, p 35.
[70] Spence, *Union,* p 246.
[71] Spence, *Independence,* p 10. The mere fact that speeches could be given on such subjects is an indication of the interest that England took in the issues of the war.
[72] LOTHIAN, p 167.
[73] Stack, *Historic Doubts,* pp 6-7.
[74] M. Bernard, *Two Lectures on the Present American War,* Oxford, 1861, p 44.
[75] Bulloch, v II, p 314.
[76] Lecky, v I, p 488.
[77] Locke, p 21.
[78] Locke, p 10.
[79] Rose Greenhow, *op.cit.,* pp 3-4.
[80] Recent Tourist, p 29.
[81] Grattan, p 15.
[82] Hope, *Bearings,* p 5.
[83] Disraeli, *Lothair,* p 378.
[84] Lecky, v I, pp 484-485.
[85] T. Weed & Others, *The Life of Thurlow Weed,* 2 vol., Boston, 1883-1884, v II, p 383. [Hereafter: Weed]
[86] LOTHIAN, pp 183-184 & 186.

Chapter Four

The Southern Gentlemen of England

We have been concerned with seeing the 'English gentlemen' of the South as the 'Southern' gentlemen of England saw them. We have been concerned with the four great appeals to Englishmen and with their response. The four streams flowed together; the flood of Southern sympathy rose and rose until it was seeping in under the doors of Westminster. The dam of Union sentiment and lethargy and inertia still held, but it seemed at various times that, now, it was about to collapse—and when it did, England would be swept into the war. In this chapter we must examine the extent and force of this torrent and, also, that which restrained and bounded it— the dam. For the contrary sympathy with the Northern cause is, by a process of elimination, a gauge to the Southern: since nearly everyone in neutral England, except perhaps the very lowest classes, took some sort of a stand on the war, maintaining it with varying degrees of vigour and passion, that which was not Northern was, in one way or another including the anti-Northern, to be reckoned as Southern.

The Bounds of the Sympathy

There were but two bases for wide-spread partisanship of the Union cause: opposition to slavery or advocacy of democracy. No one supported the United States who was not opposed to slavery—

but then all England was opposed to slavery, and was initially Northern for that reason. The more intelligent and literate classes almost
at once perceived that both more and less were involved in the struggle: the tariff and freedom of nationalities and democracy were involved; slavery, if President Lincoln were to be believed, was not.
But some Englishmen remained blind to every issue but slavery and
deaf to the disclaimers of Lincoln and others, unshakeably convinced
that the North had launched a holy crusade for the benefit of the
black man. Judged by the results, such people were right—right
for the wrong reasons, perhaps—and, after the war, they must have
been a bane to their more informed and logical fellows. Those who
favoured the North on the basis of democracy, the Radical reformers
of the Manchester School, were not at all blind to the issues. These
'democrats' of England, particularly John Bright, hated aristocracy
whether English or Southern and were the leaders of the Northern
party. This party did not include all of the Radicals, for some, like
Richard Cobden, lost their faith in the 'Model Republic' owing to
its inability to prevent civil war; others saw the right of self-
government, to which the Radicals were equally committed, as the
primary issue at stake. But the rest, the 'Radical-Yankees', as their
opponents called them, never admitted to a doubt of the victorious
virtue of democracy—indeed, it is rather likely that their early
assurance, despite every denial, that the Union was fighting to
manumit the slaves sprang more from their faith in democracy than
from the evidence.

   Although the leadership of the Northern forces was democratic
rather than abolitionist or Evangelical, there is some question as
to whether any large number of Englishmen had strong feelings for
democracy as such. There can be little doubt that, as Henry Pelling says, there was and had been for over a decade a friendliness
towards the United States in the ranks of labour[1]; but it is not clear
that this friendliness involved an active belief in democracy. Some
writers have seen all the underpriviledged of England, the lower
of the 'two nations' in Sybil, looking to American democracy as

the hope of the world.[2] But such a view assumes for the working man both a discontent and a political awareness of which there is little evidence in the early sixties. At all events, the strongly democratic leadership chose to direct their principal appeal to the universal anti-slavery sentiment. This was not, though, only a humanitarian pleading for distant black men; on the contrary, it was a suggestion, repeated again and again, that the freedom of the English working man was linked with the success of the Union crusade against slavery. Should the Confederacy win, it was implied, free-born Englishmen would be enslaved; all their hard-won gains from Magna Carta to the Bill of Rights would be swept away in the triumph of Southern ideas. "Those who hold and proclaim such sentiments as these", wrote Goldwin Smith, one of the ablest of pro-Northern propagandists, "may naturally proceed to still more extensive and startling doctrines affecting the position of the labourer, without regard to the colour of his skin, in all the countries of the world." And, more bluntly: "The American Slave-owner proposes to put an end to the freedom of labour all over the world."[3] Since so many writers after the event have imputed dishonesty only to the losing side, it may be appropriate to note in passing that all this was rather less honest than the frank upper-class hostility to the rule of the 'mob'. The point is, simply, that an appeal was necessary on some other ground than democracy *per se,* and it was discovered in the threat to the working man from aristocracy imbued with 'Southern' ideas. Thus, although the appeal was based on anti-slavery sentiment, it was to a large degree anti-aristocratic.[4]★ And it was repeated, with variations, over and over: The South is the natural enemy of free labour; the Union stands for the sanctity of labour; the progress, and indeed the very freedom, of the British worker depends on the forces of Righteousness crushing the wicked slave-holders. The North has no other purpose

★ Max Beloff says: "The pro-Northern sentiment of the radical and working-class press was anti-aristocratic rather than pro-negro."

than manumission of the slaves; the South fights solely to keep them in their chains.

But England was not quite convinced. Well-meaning people, sincerely opposed to slavery, felt that this black and white argument was an over-simplification. Some felt with Gladstone that "slavery was the calamity of the South; and that it was not for us, at any rate, to write it down as their crime."[5] Many remained doubtful as to how much, if at all, slavery had to do with the war. Not only had Lincoln denied his intention, right, or inclination to interfere with slavery, but he had removed a General Fremont from command for local emancipation in captured territory. Seward and many others had made strong statements that, regardless of the result of the struggle, slavery would remain unaffected. Slavery continued to be maintained in certain Union states, and stories were widely circulated in England about the dislike and ill-treatment of the Negro in the others. Thus,—"All examination confirms at every point the repeated emphatic declarations of President Lincoln, that the Federal States carry on this war [only] to restore the Union".[6] But, although it was far from clear that Northern victory would help the Negro, it appeared that he might benefit from Southern independence, if only in the ending of the Fugitive Slave Law. Noted supporters of the South, particularly James Spence, were saying publicly that the Confederacy would in time emancipate; and others were saying privately that the process of gradual emancipation would begin shortly after independence was established. So it was that the very hostility of Englishmen to slavery often "converted them first into opponents of the North and next into partisans of the South."[7]

One might expect Abraham Lincoln's Emancipation Proclamation on the first day of 1863 to have removed all doubt and enlisted all England in support of the Union cause. It did not do so. There were several reasons why its effect was less than might have been anticipated. In view of their earlier statements, Lincoln and his Government were clearly forsworn. Furthermore, many Englishmen knew by this time that such a measure was a violation of the Con-

stitution Lincoln was under oath to uphold. The combination of
bad faith and defeat—a fortnight before the Proclamation Lee had
so thoroughly crushed the United States army at Fredericksburg
that it was widely regarded as the decisive battle of the war—
suggested that emancipation had nothing nobler in intent than to
strike a blow by means of a servile uprising. (See again pp 67-68.)
Such a view seemed confirmed by the document itself, which, in
the words of one Englishman, "enfranchises all the slaves over
whom the United States have no authority, and keeps in bondage
all the slaves in the Border States, and those portions of the Confederate States over which the United States' armies are dominant."[8]
Some Englishmen objected to Lincoln's violating the supreme law
of his land; others who cared nothing for the law could see only
insincerity in Lincoln's not freeing the slaves in the United States.
" Very few have any faith in the anti-slavery professions of the
North," wrote an Englishman who was not a supporter of the South,
"nor has our faith been strengthened by the late proclamation."[9]
Another wrote: "This weapon was aimed as a last stroke, almost
in desperation, when defeat on every side all but overwhelmed the
Federal forces".[10] Thus it was that the Proclamation failed of its
effect in England. The United States Government had said too
much. Englishmen had had too much time to look at the problem,
not only from the legal point of view but from the point of view
of the Negro himself: many had come to believe that sudden
emancipation—quite aside from possible insurrection—might not
be in the best interests of the black man who needed a gradual in-
troduction to responsible freedom. They were, of course, right; but
the Proclamation, as they saw, was not principally concerned with
the best interests of the black man. Lincoln's action, in short, cleared
away some English doubts—and substituted others. "Both sides
found their convictions strengthened"[11]: The Manchester School
leaders supported the North and preached the crusade with greater
vigour and assurance; the friends of the South could see nothing
but 'the crowning atrocity' or 'empty hypocrisy'. Some waverers,

chiefly of the less-informed classes, were no doubt won over, but on the whole there was no great shift of sympathy as a result of the Proclamation.

One other aspect of the attitude towards slavery should be touched upon. The Southerners and some of their English supporters presented the 'peculiar institution' with considerable skill as a system which accorded the child-like blacks kindly and paternal care. There is a hint of this attitude in Thackeray's *The Virginians* well before the war, and it gained ground later. The Earl of Donoughmore said in conversation that, although he had always felt strongly on the subject of slavery, "he must admit that his opinions, so far as regarded its status in the South, had been much modified by information derived through events of the war."[12] This moderation was, to some extent, a reaction to the immoderation of the Northern agitators whose "tone assumed that all slave-holders were like the heavy villain in 'Uncle Tom's Cabin' ".[13] There was even a tendency in England to re-examine the merits of slavery. The President of the Anthropology Society of London read a paper "On the Negro's Place in Nature" in which he concluded that the Negro would not work without persuasion and that "English institutions are not suited to the Negro race."[14] Many writers arrived at the same conclusion from the decline of the West Indies.[15] There was also a turning to the Bible[16], in which slavery was accepted without condemnation, for instance, in the Epistle to Philemon where St. Paul sends the runaway slave, Onesimus, back to his master. Thus, after the Proclamation, there appeared frequently the condemning: What the Blessed Saint Paul would not do, Lincoln has done. In the England of the sixties the Biblical argument could not have been without effect. At all events, there was enough change from the crusading abolitionism of the past that a writer in 1864 could reproach his countrymen for their "very moderated tone in reference to the institution [of slavery]. . . [which] has ceased to be regarded as an intolerable wrong,. . . whilst with many, all that remains of their old abolition zeal is a decent protest".[17]

But, although confusion as to the relation of slavery to the war persisted, although the Proclamation had less effect than might have been expected, although there was something of a second look at the institution of slavery, the abolitionist sentiment continued to run deep and strong. And it was deepest and strongest in the very classes, the Nonconformists and the working men, to which Bright and his fellows made their chief plea, with the result, it is said, that the bulk of Northern sentiment was in these groups. The Anglican Evangelicals, so often on controversial issues allied with the Nonconformists, were far from agreement on this issue, partly because such leaders as Lord Shaftesbury and Bishop Wilberforce, as well as most of the clergy, were 'Southern'. The name Wilberforce must have been to many Evangelicals, and Nonconformists as well, a trustworthy guide in any matter connected with slavery, in view of his father's fight against the slave trade. A number of free-church preachers nevertheless—notably the Congregationalist Newman Hall—were resolutely Northern in sympathy. In one of his speeches Hall asked how the lack of sympathy for the North was to be explained, and then answered that it was not because of Englishmen's indifference to slavery, "but because they so deeply abhor it, many in this country have no sympathy with the North", for its victory will "rivet more tightly the fetters of the slave".[18] Those who withheld sympathy from the North on such grounds were presumably those who were won over by the Proclamation. And yet, it was in connexion with the Emancipation Proclamation that the clergymen of the Confederate States issued their *Address to Christians Throughout the World,* which must have been read by countless Nonconformists since, by a masterstroke on the part of the friends of the South, it was stitched up with every copy of the current issues of nearly all the religious journals and papers. This moving and dignified appeal, after pointing out that the slave was happy and Christian, spoke in words of solemn condemnation of the Emancipation Proclamation: "we—ministers of our Lord Jesus Christ, and members of His holy Church, . . . call heaven and earth

to record, that in the name of Him...whom we serve, *we protest!*"[19]
It was signed by many clergymen of every denomination; and it
could not have failed to carry, if not conviction, at least a ringing
sincerity—and perhaps a doubt—to churchfolk. In any case, not
one of the Nonconformist denominations came out unequivocally
for the Union; and even in 1863, after the Proclamation, the
organizers of abolition meetings in Exeter Hall refrained from iden-
tifying the cause of abolition with the cause of the North. It seems
probable that the Emancipation Proclamation did not mark the
decisive swing to the North that some historians have suggested;
and that, while the North had much support from the Nonconformists, especially after the Proclamation, they were never solidly
'Northern'.

The other large group to which John Bright addressed his efforts
was labour, which of course included many of the Nonconformists.
In dozens of histories it has been averred that the working classes
were 'sound' (i.e., Northern); that the 'great heart of Lancashire
beat for the Union'; that upsurgent democracy among the working classes kept England from intervening. This view that the working classes of the big industrial towns (the rural labourer appears
to have had no known opinions) were 'sound' requires modifica-
tion. Certainly the view was not altogether established at the time.
"The lower orders were sound, so Mr. Bright tells us," wrote a
dispassionate Englishman just after the war, "and the assertion is
as easy to make as it is hard to disprove, and we must be content
to let it rest. They certainly did not demand war to reopen the mills
of Lancashire; but the orderly behaviour, and the absence of agitation among the working classes, are the only facts from which their
sympathy with the Federal cause can be said to be deduced, and
these may have been due to other causes."[20] One such other cause
for the absence of agitation may be that their sufferings in the cotton famine have been somewhat exaggerated in the traditional accounts. Lord Stanley, writing to Disraeli in 1862 of the cotton-
manufacturing district, said: "men, women, and children seem hale

and healthy"; and again in late '63: "It is incredible how little harm has been done by the cotton famine. Even the public houses go on as usual. The truth is that the operatives living on ⅔rd of their former wages are better off than the average English labourers".[21] But other contemporary accounts leave little room for doubt that there was much real suffering in some districts; still, the sufferers did not agitate. Karl Marx, at first pleased with the English working men, later became disgusted with their "sheep's attitude" and their "christian slave nature".[22] The writer of one of the chief contemporary accounts of the cotton famine, Arnold, speaks frequently of the democratic and abolitionist sentiments among the leaders of the operatives—but it is always the leaders, not the men as a whole He quotes a song the men sang which, so far as it mentions the war, does not look like either Northern sympathies or faith in Northern victory.[23] There seems to be little evidence to support the assertion that, either before or after the Emancipation Proclamation, there was any solid or vigorous support of the Union cause among the working men. Perhaps the final blow to this legend of impassioned Lancashire loyalty to Lincoln and the Northern liberators has been dealt by F.L. Owsley. He makes it quite clear that these half-starved, "sodden, apathetic people" were purchaseable and purchased, for a few pence, by the agitators of both sides—only, the Northern group began earlier, had more pounds to spend, and, especially, had the easier task of quietening instead of rousing to indignant action.[24] In so far as Lancashiremen had opinions on the war, they were probably fairly well divided, the North having—just—an edge.★

"The North, then, were not without sympathizers in England, and I have done my best to indicate who they were [the vehement

---

★ Anne Grimshaw, "Confederates Abroad: King Cotton & Loyal Lancashire" in *The Southern Partisan* (Winter, 1984), offers substantial evidence that her home town, Oldham, in the very heart of the allegedly pro-Northern Lancashire cotton-mill region, was, in fact, full of lively sympathy for the *Confederacy*.

advocates of popular government]; I must, at the same time, say that the English sympathies with the North were over represented by the English press. The Northern partisans were zealous... but they never persuaded the English community, which looked only to the grand outlines of the case. They saw a people fighting, against fearful odds, for the independence of their country, with heroic courage and devoted patriotism, and they could not withhold their sympathies.... I appeal to this whole community [England], whether, in any chance meeting of a dozen Englishmen, that it was not more probable that there would be found no one favourer of the North, than that more than one would be found.''[25] So wrote an Englishman, Stephen Locke, with a manifest desire to tell the truth, just after the war amidst the huge reverberations of Northern victory. And there we shall leave the sympathy for the United States that bounded the sympathy for the Confederacy: the advanced Radicals, not great in number; many of the labour foremen but not a great many of the working men; many but not all the Nonconformists, though probably they were the main numerical support of the North; and, finally, a scattering of extremists of various kinds who thought that their particular views would be aided by Northern victory: free thinkers, Unitarians, temperance advocates, atheists— and, of course, Karl Marx. The Nonconformists, somewhat unreasonably, saw the North as fighting to liberate the slaves; the other groups and persons thought Northern victory would favour the progress of their ideas in England. Since it has so often been suggested that Southern sympathizers were motivated principally by hate and self-interest while the Northern were disinterested lovers of righteousness, it might in justice be pointed out that neither party were all black or all white. Some Northern supporters were idealists; others were motivated primarily by hatred of aristocracy. Similarly, some Southern supporters cared only for the discrediting of democracy, and others gave their whole sympathy to the Southerners for no other reason than that they were ''fighting, against fearful odds, for the independence of their country''.

The Extent of the Sympathy

Thàt, then, was the dam; it seems to have been none too strong a structure. If so, was the torrent a lesser thing than has been suggested? To answer that question, we must attempt to see where in England, in what groups, the Southern strength lay. First of all, with regard to labour, we have seen reason to doubt the extent and passion of its pro-Northern sympathies. On the other hand, just as there were working men with genuine pro-northern sympathies, so, there is reason to believe, there were others who sided with the South. A shrewd, contemporary, pro-Union observer commented on the effectiveness of the argument that the "Americans of the North are a mixed race. The pure English race is there, where the South is doing battle".[26] In open-air meetings, at Sheffield and other big towns, where such arguments were presented, motions of sympathy with the Confederacy were carried. A pamphleteer, who, if mistaken, was at least honest, warns Bright not to speak in the name of the working men, "nine-tenths of whom, I believe, would agree with [the Southern position]; and nine-tenths of whom, I also believe, would hold up their hands tomorrow in favour of the recognition of the South."[27] When a preacher from the United States, H. W. Beecher, toured the country in 1863 to speak for the Union, "he was all but spurned at Edinburgh, all but cursed at Glasgow," and at Liverpool, most Southern of cities, "he would have died, if one could die of such things, under a shower of groans and hisses."[28] This is rather less significant—after all, he got better receptions elsewhere—than the *kind* of interruption he experienced; much is suggested as to the ideas fixed in the English mind by these responses: At any mention of Lee or Jackson, enormous cheers. At statements of Northern kinship to England, cries of "No, no!" and "Degenerate sons!" At a reference to bringing the South back into the Union, the cry "They are Anglo-Saxon and will never come back!" And, finally, when Beecher began a sentence with a reference to the South's seeking independence, the cheering became immense and "half the audience rose to their feet, waving hats and handkerchiefs".[29] It appears probable that there was not only less Northern sentiment among the working classes than tradition has it but, as James Spence and other contemporary observers believed, rather more Southern.

There can be no doubt that the aristocracy and the upper middle class were strongly Southern. "I have reason to believe that at least five out of seven in the middle and upper classes... were favourable to the South," wrote Captain Bulloch, Confederate naval commander in Europe; and he added: "Circumstances threw me a good deal with army and navy men, and I can affirm that I never met one of either service who did not warmly sympathize with the South."[30] The scornful accounts of the Federal armies by such professional soldiers as Captain Chesney, coupled with their admiration for the Confederates, make it clear why the military men preferred the latter. The Universities were on the same side. Leslie Stephen, a Union partisan, spoke of himself as a "minority of one" at Cambridge, and his biographer confirmed that the Southerners had "a large majority in the combination rooms."[31] It was probably even larger in the common rooms of Oxford. The Church of England was predominantly Confederate, the High Church completely so. The England of clubs and society was Southern. Business England, from the London shopkeepers to the great industrialists, was the same: the hope that the war might continue 'one more year' was not indifference to the outcome. The United States Consul in Liverpool wrote after the war that he had found it almost impossible to persuade anyone to testify in connexion with Confederate ship-building, because anyone who helped the enemy of the South would be injured in a business way or would lose his employment and be unable thereafter to find a situation in that city.[32] The Confederate Commissioner, Mason, dined in 1863 at the Mansion House with a distinguished company of peers, M.P.'s, and business men; although not scheduled to speak, he responded to a call from all sides with a few words on the ties of blood and interest between his country and England. One of the important business men present wrote afterwards to a friend:—

> I was at the Mansion House last night and heard the Lord Mayor virtually recognize the South in the quietest and most inoffensive way that could be imagined. The *Times* gives a very good report of what Mr. Mason said, but no description can picture the effect of his calm and dignified delivery of these simple sentences—John Kemble as "Coriolanus" was never so grand, and Mr. Mason's pauses were eloquence itself—you might have heard a pin fall except at the tumultuous interruptions arising from sympathy and admiration. It was a scene to be remembered in one's lifetime, and something to say to my grandchildren. As I came out I rubbed shoulders with Captain Tinker, Grinnell's partner, and I said, jocularly, "Well, you see the Lord Mayor has been and gone and done it." He laughingly replied: "Oh, yes, it's all over now." Depend on it, this expression of opinion from the heart of England's middle classes must tell. It will reverberate thro' the land and find an echo—it may be, even in the North itself.[33]

If the gathering at the Lord Mayor's banquet represented the heart of the middle classes, the House of Commons was the heart of the whole governing class. The Ministry did not act to bring about recognition and the Whig Members followed their lead, and the Tories did not choose to make an issue of it. Some historians have concluded that, therefore, there was little sympathy for the South in Parliament, because "any sympathy worthy of the name must at some time have been expressed by overt act."[34] Even if this be true as a general principle, it is not true when there exist good reasons against 'overt act'. We are not (yet) concerned with why the Ministry did not act; the point is, that if the Whig Ministry and the Tory leadership were in agreement, as in fact they were, that 'the time was not yet', it would hardly be remarkable if the rank and file of the Members, whatever their sympathies, were content to wait.

Moreover, because they were awaiting a lead from the Ministry that was sure to come, they expressed their views moderately or not at all. Of one Member, keenly in sympathy with the South, it was said: "When he spoke in Parliament, Fitzgerald was so moderate that one would have hardly suspected his true feelings. And he only rarely referred to the war."[35] For this reason *Hansard's Parliamentary Debates* are not a very useful guide to the sympathies of the Members, except those of the few that were attempting to prod the Government to action. To discover the sympathies of Parliament as a whole, we must look, not at what was said on the floor but at what was said elsewhere. Mason, whose task it was to know the sympathies of governmental England, wrote: "I doubt not, a word from the Minister, suggesting that the time has arrived for Recognition, would bring a unanimous response, both from the Ministerial and Opposition benches".[36] His judgement—he estimated four-fifths of the Members to be Southern—was supported by Spence who put it at ten to one; and an M.P. wrote to Russell, who might have been expected to recognize any major distortion, that nine-tenths of the House favoured recognition.[37] Gladstone believed that most Members were friendly to the South.[38] "Of the temper of the House of Commons there is no possible doubt", wrote Louis Blanc to his readers in France, and marvelled that the Opposition failed to make it an issue since the "sympathies of England at large" were Southern and "those of the Conservative party especially having long since burst forth with a violence bordering upon the scandalous".[39]

The sympathies of Parliament, even if not expressed on the floor, were those of the nation. *The Manchester Guardian* warned that debates in the House "should not be thought to have anything to do with the sentiments and sympathies of the English people, for these were entirely with the South".[40] And the sympathy for the Confederacy transcended party lines as well as class lines. "There is no question but that the public sentiment of England is decidedly with us," wrote Mason in 1862; and two years later: "Indeed, I am satisfied that so general, almost universal, is popular sentiment in England with the South. . ."[41] Sir Leslie Stephen, who struck down *The Times* after the war with a powerful booklet on its inaccuracies, quite incidentally established in the process that the paper did not lead but rather followed public opinion: Therefore, the pronounced Southern sympathies of *The Times* represent its reading of English opinion. "I was a friend of the South before Bull's Run," wrote an M.P., "and I can now the better respect my opinion when. . . my countrymen have come over in so great a majority".[42] Louis Blanc, not a friend of the South, wrote: "I think I have already told you, and I repeat it, that the partisans of the South in England are met with everywhere. . . The North has its partisans, no doubt; but they have uphill work before them, while their adversaries have only to descend the slope. The sympathies for the North are a dam; the sympathies for the South are a torrent."[43] While Russell once asserted that Northern sympathizers were in the majority (by way of explanation, perhaps, of the Government's inaction), another M.P. won "enthusiastic cheers from the numerous audience" when he denied this assertion.[44] And Russell himself wrote in a letter: "The great majority are in favour of the South and nearly our whole people are of opinion that separation wd. be a benefit both to North & South."[45] A Union representative in England wrote that "a large majority" were Southern "in settlement and sympathy."[46] Still, the Government did not act. This is not the place to consider their reasons for inaction, but it should be said here that their failure to act is not an indication of the sentiments of the English people. "I have some hope that the people of the Confederacy do not identify the English nation with the English Government", wrote the Marquess of Lothian late in 1864. "It is a very common piece of clap-trap for those who do not go along with the policy which is pursued by their Government, to pretend that if the people were rightly appealed to they would support them. But I believe that, in this case, that clap-trap is a reality. I believe that the Confederates may feel, if it is any interest to them to do so, that if of all European Governments the English Government is the most hostile—

of all nations the English nation is the most friendly."[47]

The Force of the Sympathy

The English nation after the Confederate defeat, or those who spoke for the English nation, seemed intent to deny or forget this friendliness. In the books of later date one encounters again and again the suggestion that the sympathy for the South was a lukewarm sort of thing, more a matter of hostility to the North than genuine liking for the South. It is not true. Though Englishmen may have initially turned to the unknown South in revulsion against the North, they discovered a genuine liking and enthusiasm for that short-lived and embattled nation, quite possibly liking it better than Englishmen have *ever* liked another country.

This is implicit in dozens of contemporary accounts; but warmth of heart is rather a difficult thing to prove or measure. There were, however, certain events that caused this warmth—the force or depth of the sympathy—to be manifested. One such event was the death of Stonewall Jackson after the brilliant Confederate victory of Chancellorsville: "The partisans of the South are in mourning—Stonewall Jackson is dead. Had he been an Englishman—had he fought for the cause and under the banner of England—his loss could not have been more keenly felt. . ."[48] Perhaps never had the death of a foreign general caused so extraordinary a sensation and so profound a grief. A group of Englishmen spontaneously formed a committee to raise £500 for a heroic-size statue, saying in their appeal: "Two continents, both friend and foe, combine to mourn the premature death of General Jackson, hero and Christian."[49]★ Similarly, the earlier fall of New Orleans caused an observer in Lon-

★ 4000 guineas (£4300)—more than eight times the goal—were subscribed; the statue was begun but was not completed until after the war when it was presented to Virginia. It stands in Richmond.

don to write that "the whole town was in immense excitement as though it were an English defeat."[50] There was corresponding joy over the Seven Days and later Confederate victories, until they became the expected thing. Then when the grim tidings of Gettysburg arrived, the "news was at first received with resolute incredulity in London. . . In some of the clubs there was positive indignation that such things should even be reported."[51] England mourned, then, as a nation mourns a calamity.

Very small incidents can also be revealing: for instance, there was a dinner party which was broken up because someone took the side of the North.[52] There were cheers in the House of Commons when the CSS *Alabama*'s victories were announced.[53] An English newspaper spoke of "the holiest of causes".[54] A staunch advocate of the Union wrote of the kindling amongst the educated classes of "a passionate and almost frantic excitement of feeling, such as has not been witnessed among the same party since the war against the French Revolution; that has caused the. . .press actually to foam with fury,. . .in their attempts to keep on a level with the passions of their readers;. . .that has incited members of the British House of Peers to stand forth publicly and avow themselves leaders of a league having for its object the 'disruption' of a friendly nation".[55]

Perhaps the force of the sympathy was best shown after the final defeat, which came with such appalling suddenness. Almost overnight, its brave defense all over, the South of Lee and President Davis, of beleaguered Richmond and Commissioners to England— the Confederate States of America—was gone: not a defeated nation but a conquered province. Northern victory filled the air, and what was happening to the Southerners was almost enough to prove that they had been wrong. It was one of the most sweeping triumphs of the will of a majority over a minority that the world had ever known: the American democracy filled the western sky. The Southern sympathizers in England dispersed and were quiet. Of their sympathies they said little thereafter, and their biographers said less. This was very natural. The Confederacy was not only dead but discredited; the slaves were citizens and the North had been right all along. There never had been secession, only rebellion and treason. Jefferson Davis was in a United States prison. There was talk of hanging the traitor Lee. "He ends now", wrote Engels to Marx, "as a shabby fellow."[56]

But a few Englishmen refused to rejoice in the victory train. What they said, after the Cause of the South was irrevocably lost, indicates most truly the depth and power of the feeling for the South. "Madam," said one of them to a hostile Northerner, "it is true that there were many in England who felt towards the South, just as the schoolboy feels, while he reads Homer's 'Iliad', about Hector, when he finds him battling manfully against destiny and a host of heroes."[57] A baronet who had lost £ 180,000 in Confederate bonds wrote: "I at least was not ashamed of the cause in which I lost it, nor sought to fall away from my friends when that cause came to its worst....I stood loyally by the Southern people from first to last,...I believed, and still believe, [that cause] to have been a just one."[58] Stephen Locke, whose pamphlet on English sympathies, written in 1866 with manifest sincerity and some emotion, has often been quoted in these pages, concludes his little work: "I am deeply sensible how incompetent I am to give adequate expression to the sentiments of the great body of my countrymen on this deplorable subject; but I am not without hope, that what I have said may help to awaken others (better qualified) to tell the world, that justice and humanity are not dead among us; that we hate unjust wars, abhor wars carried on with exceptional barbarity; that we hate oppression, from whatever quarter it comes, and sympathize with its victims; more especially when they have been the heroic contenders for the independence of their country."[59] A generous English nobleman pressed General Lee to come to England as his lifetime guest.[60] Disraeli caused his generous fictional nobleman to say of the Southern Colonel: "It is not unlikely that he may have lost his estates now; but that makes no difference to me. I shall treat him and all Southern gentlemen, as our fathers treated the emigrant nobility of France."[61] Lord Acton, lifelong crusader for freedom, wrote sixteen years after the surrender of the Confederacy that certain news gave him a "heartier joy... than I have been able to feel at any public event since I broke my heart over the surrender of Lee."[62] The depth of his emotion was perhaps explained in his letter to General Lee, long before, in which he said that Lee was fighting the battles of English freedom and civilization, and concluded: "I mourn for the stake which was lost at Richmond more deeply than I rejoice over that which was saved at Waterloo."[63]

This was English sympathy for the Southern Confederacy: it was a flood both wide and deep; it swept against the dam with a force sufficient, it would seem, to sweep that apparently fragile structure away. And England had but to lift her hand...

1. Pelling, *op.cit.*, p 2 ff.
2. Frank Thistlethwaite, "America & the Two Nations of Englishmen", in *The Virginia Quarterly Review,* XXXI (Autumn, 1955), pp 505-525.
3. Goldwin Smith, *Does the Bible Sanction Slavery?,* Oxford & London, 1863, p iv & p 84.
4. Max Beloff, "Great Britain & the American Civil War", *History,* XXXVII (February 1952), p 44.
5. Quoted by John Bigelow, *Lest We Forget: Gladstone, Morley and the Cotton Loan of 1863,* New York, 1905, p 36.
6. Civis Anglicus, *A Voice from the Motherland Answering Mrs. H. Beecher Stowe's Appeal,* London, 1863, p 17.
7. Justin McCarthy, p 292.
8. Hope, *Bearings,* p 12.
9. F.W. Gibbs, *Recognition: a Chapter from the History of the North American & South American States,* London, 1863, p 46.
10. Civis Anglicus, *op.cit.,* p 38.
11. John Watts, *op.cit.,* p 106.
12. Mason, p 561.
13. M. D. Conway, *Autobiography,* 2 vol., London, 1904, v I, p 363.
14. James Hunt, *On the Negro's Place in Nature,* London, 1863, pp 57-58.
15. See, for examples: A. C. Brice, *Indian Cotton Supply...for Relief to Lancashire,* Cornhill, 1863; W.F. Fergusson, *The Dearth of Cotton, &c.,* London, 1863.
16. See, for examples: Bishop John H. Hopkins, *The Bible View of American Slavery,* London, 1863; Onesimus Secundus, *The True Interpretation of the American Civil War &c.,* London, 1863; and (fn 1, p 82) a reply.
17. A. Rooker, *Does it Answer? Slavery in America, a History,* London, 1864, p 3.
18. Newman Hall, *The American War, a Lecture to Working Men,* London, 1862, pp 22-23.
19. The Clergy of the Confederate States of America, *Address to Christians Throughout the World,* London, 1863, p 11.
20. Kennaway, p 266.
21. The Disraeli Papers (Letters 4 September 1862 & 31 October 1863) quoted by W. D. Jones, "The British Conservatives & the American Civil War" in *The American Historical Review,* LVIII (April 1953)3, pp 527-543, p 540.
22. Karl Marx & F. Engels, *The Civil War in the United States,* London, [1938], pp 261-262. (NB Originally articles in New York & Vienna papers 1861-62, & correspondence 1861-66, collected and edited by Richard Emmale in 1938.)
23. R.A. Arnold, *The History of the Cotton Famine,* London, 1864, pp 228, 113, & 472.
24. Owsley, pp 188-196 & 565-566.
25. Locke, pp 20-21.
26. Louis Blanc, 2ndSer., v I, p 185.

27 Nemo, *op.cit.,* p 9.
28 Louis Blanc, 2ndSer., v II, p 72 & p 66.
29 H. W. Beecher, *American Rebellion,* Report of Speeches Delivered at Public Meetings, Manchester, 1864, pp 70, 81, 40, &c.
30 Bulloch, v I, p 294, & v II, p 303.
31 F. W. Maitland, *Life & Letters of Leslie Stephen,* London, 1906, pp 123 & 107.
32 T. H. Dudley, *op.cit.,* pp 17-18.
33 T. M. Mackay of T. M. Mackay & Co., Black Ball Line, quoted by Mason, pp 391-392.
34 W. D. Jones, *op.cit.,* pp 527-528.
35 *Ibid.,* p 533 fn.
36 Mason, pp 370 & 405.
37 E. D. Adams, v II, p 174, & v I, p 305 fn.
38 *Hansard,* 3rdSer., CLXXI, 1800-12.
39 Louis Blanc, 2ndSer., v I, pp 121-122, & Louis Blanc, v II, p 320.
40 Quoted earlier in Prologue, see p 2.
41 Mason, pp 313 & 501.
42 Hope, *Bearings,* pp 4-5.
43 Louis Blanc, v II, p 178.
44 Louis Blanc, 2ndSer., v II, p 71.
45 W. D. Jones, *op.cit.,* p 529 (quoting Russell to Lyons 19 July 1862).
46 Weed, v I, p 649.
47 LOTHIAN, pp 221 & 223.
48 Louis Blanc, 2nd Ser., v I, p 153.
49 Mason, pp 426 & 429.
50 *A Cycle of Adams Letters* (Henry Adams), p 146.
51 Justin McCarthy, v III, p 327.
52 R. H. Dana, *The "Trent" Affair, an Aftermath,* Cambridge, Mass., 1912, p 14.
53 J. E. Cairns, *England's Neutrality in the American Contest,* London, 1864, p 5.
54 Louis Blanc, 2ndSer., v I, p 258.
55 Goldwin Smith, *Letter to a Whig Member of the S.I.A.,* London, 1864, pp 67-68. (The 'league' was the Southern Independence Association.)
56 Marx & Engels, *op.cit.,* p 275.
57 F. B. Zincke, *Last Winter in the United States,* London, 1868, p 26.
58 Bigelow, *op.cit.,* p 21, quoting Sir Henry de Houghton, Bart.
59 Locke, p 26.
60 Freeman, *Lee,* v IV, p 208.
61 Disraeli, *Lothair,* p 200.
62 H. Paul, Ed., *Letters of Lord Acton to Mary, Daughter of the Right Hon. W. E. Gladstone,* London, 1904, pp 81-82.
63 Freeman, *Lee,* v IV, p 517.

Part III Floodgate

Chapter Five

The Defeat

Chapter Six

The Illusion

Chapter Five

The Defeat

England did not lift her hand. Because she failed to act to ensure Southern independence, the Confederate States were defeated. It is as nearly certain as anything that never happened can be that timely intervention by England would have established the Confederate States, just as timely intervention by France had established the United States. In the defeat of the Southerners, their English supporters were defeated. But is it just to say England 'failed' to act, with its implication of action both probable and expected? One does not fail to run a race who never dreamt of competing. And only if the question is answered in the affirmative, can we pose the further question: Why, then, did England fail to act? This chapter is designed to answer the earlier question, whether it is fair to say that England 'failed' to act. To answer it, we must examine a moment of fateful hesitation in England; and the consequences of that hesitation in the South; and finally the effect of the Southern defeat upon England.

The Curious Hesitation

In 1862 the Southerners were not defeated, and England had no thought that they ever would be; indeed, they looked very like winning, perhaps before the year was out. At the outbreak of war England had proclaimed a proper neutrality whilst waiting to see whether the Union armies would in fact quickly destroy the rebellion of 'a few wicked conspirators'. But now in the late summer of 1862 Lee had won the great victory of the Seven Days, and in September Lee and Jackson brilliantly defeated the United States army at the old Manassas battlefield. The North, said *The Times,* was on the 'verge of ruin'.

The balance of the bayonets was plainly falling on the Southern side. In England everyone knew that recognition of the Confederate States and, even, intervention were more than a possibility. Many looked for Ministerial action daily. Powerful men, who believed that the traditional English way of life would be endangered by a Northern success, endeavoured to force the Cabinet to ensure Southern independence. Others, deeply stirred by the valiant struggle of the South, urged Englishmen to help her as they had helped Greece and Italy. Countless appeals stressed the same points: The Southerners, our kinsmen, have proved by their indomitable spirit that they are worthy of independence; England must abide her traditions and assist them. "I declare that the cause of the South is the cause of freedom", wrote A. J. B. Beresford Hope, "the cause of those principles of constitutional government which we desire to see prevailing all over the world. . . . If we made allowances for Italy, should we not be willing to make equal allowances for our own flesh and blood. . . who are trying to raise up a new English nation. . . They have passed the Red Sea—shall we never give them a hand that they may reach the promised land?"[1] Such an appeal was not easy to resist, or to discredit. Louis Blanc wrote: "I say. . . without hesitation, because I think it to be a fact, that everything here [in England] is preparing for a signal recognition of the Southern States."[2] Louis Blanc was not mistaken; the Government were seriously considering recognition and mediation.

The question of recognition and mediation had in fact been turned over from the beginning: the Government were not as hostile as Lord Lothian suggested, but they were waiting for the right moment. Gladstone, a true Liberal, sympathized with the South on the grounds that it was struggling as an oppressed nationality. Palmerston was at once sympathetic to the South and hostile to the North. Even Russell, if not in favour of the Confederacy, had small sympathy with its enemies. Other members of the Cabinet, for various reasons, regarded the separation of the former regions as desirable. In September, 1862, the right moment came. The Federals had got a "very complete smashing" at the second battle of Manassas (or Bull Run); and General Lee then led the Army of Northern Virginia across the frontiers of the United States. Palmerston wrote to Russell that, if the Union suffered another great defeat, if Washington or Baltimore should fall, it would be time to mediate. "I agree," replied Russell, adding that, if the North refused mediation, England should recognize the independence of the Confederacy. Gladstone also agreed, enthusiastically, and urged that there be no delay lest Lancashire should riot (the Southern forces at this moment were doing nothing to rouse the shire). The 'Triumvirate' were united; it seemed that nothing could halt the recognition so eagerly sought by the Confederates. In Maryland Lee fought the great and indecisive battle of Sharpsburg (or Antietam): if, tactically, it was a Confederate victory, it was a strategic defeat, for Lee withdrew the army into Virginia. Unchecked by this intelligence, Lord Russell continued to plan mediation. And Gladstone shook the country by implying unmistakably that recognition was at hand when he said, in the famous Newcastle speech, that Jefferson Davis had not only made an army and a navy but had made a *nation*.

When Gladstone told the "wildly cheering crowd"[3] that President Davis had made a nation, he did but say what he and most of England believed: that a nation had, in fact, come permanently into being. And in foreshadowing recognition, "he but re-echoed the sentiment prevailing in the minds of the people".[4] *The Spectator,* Northern in sympathy, said: "We cannot, bitterly as we lament the decision, honestly blame the Cabinet. They have only followed the lead of the people, and followed it at far distance. The educated million in England, with here and there an exception, have become unmistakably Southern. . . . The Cabinet is not to blame if, after enforcing delay sufficient for reconsideration, it obeys the national will."[5] Louis Blanc, far from disagreeing with *The Spectator* about the national will, was inclined to suspect that Gladstone had "yielded to the temptation of courting popularity" by appealing to the universal Southern feeling; Gladstone's words, he said, "went straight to the heart of the nation" which responded with a great cry of "Down with the North! The South for ever!"[6]

The Spectator also said: "the Cabinet has made up its mind that the American struggle is over, and that henceforward two nations must exist on the American continent."[7] It was, in fact, a favourable moment, the 'right moment', for, as Gladstone had observed in his Memorandum to the Cabinet: "fortunes have been placed for the moment *in equilibrio* by the failure of the main invasions on both sides".[8] But the Cabinet had not made up its mind, despite Gladstone and the enthusiastic English reaction; Lord Palmerston hesitated, feeling that this was not the 'right moment'; Gladstone and Russell, who felt that it was, probably agreed that a better one would come along. But this was the moment of destiny; this was the flood tide of the Confederacy, and England's nearest approach to decisive action. The Government did not ever decide that there would be no action; they merely did not ever decide that it was time to act. They waited for the right moment—which was not to come again. And Parliament waited for the Ministry's lead. And England waited upon the Parliament. And France waited to follow England.

What this rather dramatic incident shows so clearly, from the "wildly cheering crowd" at Newcastle to *The Spectator*'s acceptance of what it deplored—"the national will", is the sure belief of England, held on the whole calmly and with approval, that sooner or later, at the right moment, led by 'Pam' supported by a majority of both parties in Parliament, the nation would take action—mediation, recognition, or intervention—to sustain the South. Such action was both probable and expected, and it *is,* therefore, just to say that England 'failed' to act. But then, of course, it was by no means clear that such action was necessary.

The Incredible Defeat

The Confederate States prosecuted the war with vigour and splendid courage. They had magnificent officers and devoted men. They controlled a huge area with many defensive advantages. Rarely, if ever, in history has a revolutionary cause possessed so many trained leaders or a government so thoroughly organized. Rarely has one been so blessed by fumbling on the part of the enemy. The Thirteen Colonies had neither the vigour and unanimity nor the patriotism nor the able officers of the Southern Confederacy, and yet against the might of England they won their independence. Thinking men everywhere regarded the conquest of the Confederacy as an impossibility—even if England did not intervene, in itself an impossibility should the war continue for more than a few months. What factors were neglected in such thinking? Why did the Confederacy fail?

A complete answer is not within the scope of this work. Many theories have been advanced with which we are little concerned: theories explaining the defeat in terms of fundamentally mistaken strategy, of too much state rights, of too much Presidential interference in military affairs, or of the slow strangulation of the Union blockade.★ And this is but a partial list. Then there are the tiny, jeweled turning-points of history: General Longstreet's fatal hesitation at Gettysburg; the lost order that disclosed Lee's plan of march into Maryland; the absence of Stuart and the cavalry at a critical juncture. A better Southern strategy might only have forced the emergence of a Northern general to meet it. Victories in Maryland or Pennsylvania might have won the war if the state-rights

★ The blockade theory of Southern defeat, advanced by C. F. Adams, Jr, has, in my opinion, been quite demolished by F. L. Owsley.

peace party in the North were strong enough; or just as well, might have caused the Union to gird itself for a supreme effort. It is true, no doubt, as de Tocqueville says, that an aristocracy must strike early and hard to win—but whether the South could have struck earlier or harder is in doubt. The fact remains, the United States were much more powerful in every respect, men, ships, wealth. More important, they were a partially industrialized nation and could draw, as the South could not, upon the factories of England. A huge industrial democracy waging total war upon a much smaller agrarian aristocracy—after all, it is not so very incredible that the South should have lost.

And yet, by the genius of Lee and Jackson, it almost won. It looked like winning, certainly; and the watching world did not take into account the power of steam—not even England which knew something about that power. And not the South. She faced the prospect, and then the actuality, of war with a comfortable assurance hugged to her breast: that England must intervene to get cotton. It was a logical certainty, shared by most of the world—perhaps more logical and far less naive than Marxian determinism—but it turned out to be illusory. The South, too, had a glittering illusion.

Had England intervened, the Confederacy or, rather, 'the Allies' would in all probability have won: and, in the result, not otherwise.★ As the Thirteen Colonies won through French intervention: and not otherwise. W. E. H. Lecky, in contrasting the "incomparably higher level of courage, tenacity, and self-sacrifice" of the Southern states as opposed to the Thirteen Colonies, spoke of the latter's "entire dependence for success on foreign assistance".[9] That is the essential difference between the outcomes of the two wars for independence: in the one France acted (as, indeed, she wished to do in the 1860's); in the other England did not act. And yet, ironically, one reason for English certainty that the Confederacy

---

★ We shall see in the Epilogue what might have followed English intervention.

would win without help was that the Thirteen Colonies had won—
with help.

England's failure to act, far more than Gettysburg, was the main
lost battle of the Confederacy, a battle waged by Southerners and
their English friends in Westminster and in the shires. English intervention was probable and expected and, in the event, utterly
necessary. It was also, from the South's point of view, wholly
desirable. That it was equally desirable from England's own point
of view is rather less clear.

The Unpardonable Blunder

"England committed the unpardonable blunder, from her point
of view," wrote a Prussian general, "of not supporting the Southern
States in the American War of Secession."[10] Is the statement true,
or partly true? Would England's best interests have been served by
her establishing the Confederate States? Was it an 'unpardonable
blunder' not to have done so? These are difficult, if not impossible, questions. Certainly there are few English historians today, if
any, who regard England's neutrality as a blunder in the sense that
they regard certain policies of George III's Government as blunders,
for instance, or Allied passivity to the rise of Hitler as a blunder.

It may fairly be assumed that the 'Triumvirate' could have carried the Parliament and the nation with them if they had decided
to act. And France would very willingly have coöperated. It also
seems nearly certain that England and France together, or England
alone, could have established the independence of the Confederacy,
especially at the 'right moment' in 1862 when the Southern arms
were everywhere victorious. Indeed, as Lord Palmerston said, it
would be "not perhaps a very formidable thing for England and
France combined."[11] Max Beloff has suggested a number of consequences of English action: "Had Great Britain intervened, as
seemed quite possible at more than one juncture, the new era of

understanding and intermittent collaboration which began at the turn of the century would hardly have come about. . . . The North and South would have separated for an indefinite period; the North would have conquered Canada; and the setting-up in Mexico of a French puppet empire would have set aside the Monroe Doctrine.''[12] It seems doubtful that the North and South would ever have reunited, had the Confederacy gained independence; indeed, an accession of the Confederacy to the British Empire might, of the two, have been more probable. The French puppet empire might, for various reasons, not have endured very long. As to Canada, it seems possible that England might have dispatched troops there, as she began to do at the time of the *Trent* crisis, before actually engaging in the war; and the United States, confronted with England and France and the very able armies of the Confederacy, might have been unable to conquer Canada. It is very difficult to say. At all events, it may be recalled that the England of the sixties did not greatly value Canada; indeed, Sir Henry Taylor, an official of the Colonial Office wrote to the Duke of Newcastle in 1864 that the worst result of the war between the American states was that of involving England and Canada "in closer relations and a common cause"—that is, in postponing their separation.[13] An even more speculative point is that which concerns the "new era of understanding and intermittent collaboration" between Great Britain and the United States in the twentieth century. If, in fact, Anglo-American co-operation is based on common political beliefs, then the new era might have come about in any case, though a bit later. In the meantime, all through the latter nineteenth century indeed, there would surely have been a new era of understanding and close collaboration between Great Britain and the grateful Confederate States. The economic advantages arising from and cementing this relationship have been shown on earlier pages. It is rather too speculative to consider what might have followed from the triumph of the state rights principle, the defeat of which Lord Acton so deeply mourned. But it might be suggested that the long-range result of

England's having sustained the Confederacy could have been to make the co-operation of the English-speaking world *less* difficult and more a consultation among equals. From the point of view of England, it is far from clear that intervention would have had injurious consequences to her international position or to her Empire; it seems quite probable that the advantages might have outweighed the disadvantages.

The Russian Ambassador to Washingon, writing to Prince Alexander Gorchakov in 1861 after the secession of most of the deep South, said: "Great Britain seems to enjoy a stroke of fortune rare in history. She alone will profit by the destruction of the United States..."[14]

The international results of English policy, however, are only part of the whole. Some of the most outspoken supporters of the South—like the leaders of the Northern party also—were concerned with democracy: an evil or a blessing. The more extreme Radicals actually hoped to see a republic in England; and all of them regarded democracy—which meant American democracy—as a panacea for every ill. Before the war there were two views of democracy: the 'panacea' of the Manchester School Radicals; and the 'danger to the nation' of their opponents. When the war came, it was well understood by both parties that American democracy, which is to say *democracy,* was on trial. There could be no return to the old two views; that was tacitly understood. But it *was* a trial. The issue was not settled. Then the United States overwhelmed the Confederacy, and American democracy ran from the Great Lakes to the Gulf of Mexico. Two years later the Reform Bill of 1867 was passed and might have been passed sooner but for loyalty to Lord Palmerston. Can it be said that the Reform Bill was the direct result of Northern victory? Few historians have gone so far, although Henry Pelling says that the victorious Union "played its part in setting Britain further and more decisively upon the path that led to full democracy." But he also says, in remarking that America as a synonym for democracy figured largely in the struggle, that

Reform "was purely an issue of British internal politics", which perhaps denies that it was an issue settled on the Virginian battlefields.[15] At all events, it is hardly an accepted proposition that the vindication of American democracy by victory was necessary for the passage of the second Reform Bill.

But if democracy was on trial in the war, then it had precisely *not* proved itself until the judgement was arrived at by combat. What if the South had won?—would the Reform Bill still have been passed, or even introduced, in the two years following 1865? The Radical leaders who had loudly proclaimed, what virtually no one else could believe, that the United States would win, would have been silenced and discredited. As it was, their opponents were silenced: *their* great argument had been that a large democracy could not survive; they had quoted de Tocqueville to predict the break-up of the Republic; and then, upon secession, had proclaimed the fulfillment of the prophecy. Democracy had not been able to prevent civil war and disintegration; it was corrupt; half of the Republic was now aristocratic. It was a damning indictment: even Radicals were discouraged. John Bright kept his faith in Northern and democratic triumph, but he could scarcely have kept it intact after Southern victory. While the Confederacy stood, the dangers inherent in democracy were demonstrated. And if democracy were a danger to the state, if it led to tyranny (France) or disintegration (America), who would be so mad as to introduce it to England? To a very large extent, the arguments and reputations of both parties depended, as surely as the Union itself, on the balance of the bayonets. But when the balance fell, when democracy proved itself—as none could appreciate better than the England of Darwin—by survival, then England's very disbelief in the possibility of such a victory distinguished democracy as the decisive element in the outcome. In precisely the same way, it would have been democracy discredited and culpable if the Union had failed. It is almost, if not quite, impossible to believe that in such event there could have been any reform in the sixties. If no reform bill could have been passed in the face of Northern defeat, then Northern victory *was* the decisive factor in the success of the bill that was passed. One cannot go beyond reform in the sixties as an issue of the war. A bill might have been passed in the next decade or two; or it might not. If the movement towards increased democracy had been checked and to some extent discredited by the discrediting of the model democracy, the next step might have been determined by further developments in the United States and the Confederate States.

A large majority of the governing classes of England were in sympathy with the South. Many of these Englishmen appreciated very well that tremendous questions were at issue. Men like Beresford Hope and Lord Robert Cecil made no mistake in what they saw. They understood what would follow a Northern victory, and they did not like it. And these men, the governing classes, were 'England'. Their best interests, and thus, in the sense we have been using the word, *England's* best interests, would have been served by England's sustaining the South, and so preventing the reform they dreaded.

This is as far as we can go towards answering the question whether, from her own point of view, England blundered in not intervening. England today, to some degree the product of non-intervention and the resultant increase of democracy, does not call it a blunder; but from the point of view of the England of nearly a century ago, it *was* perhaps the 'unpardonable blunder'.★ Max Beloff, speaking of "the wave of democratic sentiment" that followed Northern victory, and of Lord Palmerston's role in keeping England neutral, adds: "Yet it could be argued that Lord Robert Cecil had seen further into things."[16]

★ This is perhaps a needlessly difficult way of putting it, but England's non-intervention can only be justified or condemned from the values of the England that failed to intervene. Historians call non-intervention fortunate; but, had England intervened, quite possibly historians of the world that would have followed would call intervention fortunate. Almost all Americans agree that it is, after all, best that the North won; but in the sixties Carolinians and Virginians were not yet 'Americans'. Had they won, their grandchildren would shoot rockets to celebrate the fact.

It is singularly appropriate to this study that the last official flag of the Confederate States of America should have been hauled down, not in Virginia or Carolina or Mississippi but in England where so much that was vital to the continued national existence of the embattled South happened or failed to happen. Liverpool, the most Confederate city outside the CSA, was the scene. General Lee surrendered the Army of Northern Virginia at Appomattox on the ninth of April, 1865; and the other armies shortly thereafter: the nation ceased to exist. Only—not quite. In the North Pacific the Confederate armed cruiser CSS *Shenandoah* was still cheerfully sinking American ships. *Shenandoah*—the name means Daughter of the Stars—was a fast, graceful, ship-rigged vessel that had carried the Confederate flag round the world; and her young officers, among whom was a nephew of General Lee, knew nothing of the ending of their country's fight for independence. On June 28th, two and a half months after Appomattox, in the last armed action of the war, *Shenandoah* captured ten Yankee whaling ships and, crowding the crews on two of them, burnt the other eight in a spectacular finale of the great struggle. Feeling right pleased with their haul, the ship's company sailed southward towards San Francisco, which the captain and chief officer were planning to capture. This quite probably they could have done, but in August they learnt from a British vessel, not only that the war was over but that they themselves would, if captured, almost certainly be hanged as pirates by the vengeful victors. Accordingly, the now very lonely *Shenandoah* sailed south, trusting in her speed to escape any American warships that might be sighted—sailed southward down the long reaches of the South Pacific, rounded the Horn, and set her course for England, a voyage of 17,000 miles without touching land. Then in November, seven long months after Appomattox, the last flag of the Confederacy streaming from her gaff, CSS *Shenandoah* entered the port of Liverpool. There at last, with the grey-uniformed officers standing at attention on the quarterdeck, and tears on the bronzed faces of some, the order was given to haul down the colours; and the last unit of the armed forces of a conquered nation ceased to exist.

In Oxford the news of the fall of the Confederacy caused Philip Worsley, poet and Fellow of Corpus Christi College, speaking for many educated Englishmen, to write:

> No nation rose so white and fair,
> None fell so pure of crime.

What followed United States victory, in England and North America and the world, may be in fact good or bad or neither—and none of these simply because it happened—but to the English who sympathized with the South, with whom we are concerned, it was bad. They saw the importance of sustaining the South quite clearly. They were the majority of the governing classes of England. They did not merely hope, they calmly expected to recognize the independence of the South. They were 'England', and they had much to gain and more to lose. Why, then, did England—fighter of wars for far less—fail to act?

[1] Hope, *Bearings,* pp 5-6 & 42.

[2] Louis Blanc, v I, p 263.

[3] P. Guedalla, Ed., *Gladstone & Palmerston,* London, 1928, p 64.

[4] Kennaway, p 269.

[5] Rhodes, v IV, p 340.

[6] Louis Blanc, v II, pp 176-178.

[7] Rhodes, v IV, p 340.

[8] P. Guedalla, Ed., *op.cit.,* p 244.

[9] The passage is quoted more fully on p 79.

[10] General von Bernhardi quoted by W. A. Dunning, *The British Empire and the United States,* London, 1914, p xxxii.

[11] E. Ashley, *The Life of Henry John Temple, Viscount Palmerston, 1846-1865,* 2 vol., London, 1876, v II, p 210.

[12] M. Beloff, *op.cit.,* p 40.

[13] H. Duncan Hall, *The British Commonwealth of Nations,* London, 1920, pp 50-51.

[14] Paul Gottfried, "Through European Eyes", *The Southern Partisan,* Summer 1985.

[15] Pelling, *op.cit.,* p 29 & p 10.

[16] Beloff, *op.cit.,* pp 47-48.

Chapter Six

The Illusion

It is a just question: Why did England fail to act? We have seen that the flood of Southern sympathy was great enough, and the stakes were great enough, to make it appear as a virtual certainty that England would sustain Southern independence—by mediation and recognition and, if necessary, by intervention. Why did the flood fail to sweep away the fragile-seeming dam of Northern sentiment supported by inertia? It is customary now to say that the dam was far, far stronger than anyone knew at the time. And, indeed, if it withstood the torrent, it must have been. Unless there was a way to reduce the pressure on the dam. There were many reasons, both long-range and short-range ones, to urge action, as we have seen, and other reasons, as we shall see, to support inaction. But it is the principal purpose of this chapter to show that there was a floodgate, which, quite simply and unobtrusively, drew off the force of the sympathy, preventing there ever being pressure enough to carry away the dam—which, otherwise, could not have stood.

The Improbable Inaction

There were apparently compelling reasons for England to take such action as would ensure Confederate independence. But there were also reasons, presumably more compelling, to persuade her to inaction. In order to examine these latter—most of which have, at one time or another, been proposed as the main reasons—our point of view must be, not that of Englishmen in general or of the educated million but that of government, for it was the Government which must have initiated action. We are concerned less with that particular Government which did in fact hold office during the war than with any Government that might have been in office at the time. Actually, though, that particular Ministry, from the Prime Minister and the Foreign Secretary to the middle-class Liberal members, may have had much to do with inaction. The key figure is, of course, Lord Palmerston; he it was who hesitated in 1862 after initiating the idea that the right moment was approaching. According to Beloff, Lord Palmerston, far more than John Bright, is the man who, firmly in control of the situation, was responsible for England's continued neutrality.[1] That Ministry might have carried England into war on the strength of the existing English sympathy for the South, or on less; but they probably could not have withstood a more vigorous demand for intervention.

First of all, there were what might be called negative reasons for inaction. The two paramount concerns of British foreign policy—the command of the sea and the European balance of power—were unaffected by the war in America. The powerful cotton lords were making no real demand for cotton; and the dangerous unrest among the Lancashire operatives, although expected and even dreaded, had not appeared. In another era, either earlier or later, there might have been an inclination to win back for the Empire the former Southern Colonies, but in the 'Little England' of the sixties, when minds were dominated by the coming triumph of free trade along with general colonial independence, the Empire was little valued, and such an idea could not be seriously entertained in England. ★ These several imperatives to action did not operate.

Certain attitudes of mind that existed at the time form another

★ For reason to suppose that the idea was entertained in the South and that Southerners even hinted that Barkis was willing, see Appendix.

group of reasons that have been proposed for inaction. One may be mentioned only to be dismissed: the dislike of war among free-traders and Evangelicals. While genuine, it was neither wide-spread nor deep-rooted enough to alter national policy.★ The same may be said of faith in democracy: it existed, it was genuine and ardent, but there were not enough democrats to keep England inactive. Much more important than either was hostility to slavery: the inaction has often been attributed to the abolitionist sentiment of England, or of Lancashire alone; it has even, to bring it to a point, been attributed to the influence of one woman—Harriet Stowe. There is little question of the reality, though some question of the vigour, of the anti-slavery feeling; we have, in any case, seen reason to doubt its leading invariably, or even usually, to partisanship of the North. Its importance is not always clearly seen. It did not put England in the Northern camp; it did not keep England from being in the Southern camp. What it *did* do was to create a certain reluctance, partly a matter of 'face' in view of England's abolitionist past, to be in open alliance with a slave-owning power until or unless it was necessary. This reluctance to initiate action until it could be done without England's seeming too eager (e.g., after the capture of Washington) gave a special importance to the 'right moment'.

A third and significant group contains the economic reasons of a positive nature. Again, one is of small importance: the 'King Wheat' theory, advanced first by Marx, that England's dependence upon Northern wheat enforced neutrality. Since there were other sources which England could, and later did, turn to for wheat, the theory collapses. But other economic reasons (discussed in Chapter III) were of much importance: There was the continuing destruction by Confederate cruisers of the only mercantile marine that rivalled England's; wars have been fought to gain less than was being gained by inaction. Many cotton lords were being saved from the ruin that had impended because of the glut of manufactured

★ "When there was peace, he was for peace; when there was war, he went."

goods; and they entertained a (vain) hope that adequate cotton would soon be forthcoming from India. Finally, there were the big profits being made as a direct result of the war by the woollen and linen manufacturers, the ship builders and armament makers, and many others. To at least one historian—and the one who has looked most clear-sightedly at these matters, the late F. L. Owsley—war profits are the key to England's inaction. And certainly it is true that the cotton situation, the activities of the CSS *Alabama* and her sisters, and the war profits, all combined to suggest powerfully to Englishmen, if not inaction, at least no action for the present. In the end, if not in men's minds, there may not be much difference.

Under the heading 'fear' or 'timidity' may be grouped the last of the outstanding reasons for inaction: England did not act, it is said, because, owing to the foaming belligerency of United States Secretary of State Seward and the skilled bluffing of United States Minister Adams, the Ministry were afraid. This is shown by Adams' forcing Lord Russell, despite his insistence that there was no basis in English law for such action, to stop the sailing of the iron-clad rams destined for the Confederacy. Adams' memorable threat to Russell is often quoted: "It would be superfluous in me to point out to your Lordship that this is war." But Russell had already halted the rams. There were real reasons for a certain hesitation in under-taking war with the United States which included the vulnerability of Canada and of, especially, the English mercantile marine which would be exposed to the same sort of destruction as that overtaking the American. Yet England feared for Canada in any event; and armed intervention with both France and the Confederacy as allies might have ensured a short war with relatively little damage to the mercantile marine and with in the end a greater security for Canada than otherwise appeared probable. The battle in Hampton Roads between the iron-clads, the USS *Monitor* and the CSS *Virginia,* and the latter's sinking several powerful wooden warships, is said to have caused Great Britain qualms for her Navy in the event of war. This is unlikely, for she had powerful ironclads of her own, as did France, and could easily outbuild the United States. England undoubtedly entertained dark suspicions of the designs of France, yet the Ministry must have been fully aware that Napoleon was genuinely anxious to bolster up his Mexican empire by co-operating in mediation or intervention. English influence on the Continent would have been temporarily lessened by an American war: but she was, in any case, unable to halt the Prussian attack on Denmark or the Russian on Poland; and her rival, France, would be equally preoccupied in America. Finally, it has been suggested that the Queen's ill health and nervous dread of war caused the Ministry to hesitate. It is quite certain that England was not as fearful as all this suggests. At the time of the *Trent* affair the Editor of *The Times* wrote to Russell that "the whole Army, Navy, and Volunteers are of one mind and all mad for service in America. For once, the Navy has been found ready when wanted; as to the Army, we might recruit each company into a battalion if necessary."[2] The truth is, again to quote Lord Palmerston, that a war with the remaining United States, already hard beset by the Southern armies, would have been: "not perhaps a very formidable thing for England and France combined."[3] Probably Seward and Adams did convince the Cabinet that the United States would go to war very readily, possibly over recognition of the Confederate States. The effect of this conviction, however, was not to cause the Ministry to fear intervention. The effect was to keep them from offering mediation until they were prepared to extend recognition; and to keep them from extending recognition until they were prepared for the war that might follow. Thus in the affair of the Confederate rams, the Government, unless they were prepared to intervene in any event, would not risk an unintended war over the rams. The Northern belligerency (supported by the reluctance to be in open alliance with a slave-owning nation unless it were 'necessary') had one important effect: the unmistakable chip on the Yankee shoulder ensured that England would not 'drift' into the war by easy stages. But that was all; it was not in itself responsible for England's inaction.

No one of these reasons or no one group, nor all of them put together, caused the improbable inaction; one more must be added, the most important of all. There were very great reasons on the other side which urged action. There were also sheer admiration and sympathy which caused Englishmen to wish to help the South and do justice to the Southerners by recognition. It is in general true that the English governing class has been realistic rather than sentimental with regard to foreign policy; but there was here a coincidence of cold-blooded realism about their own best interests and warm-hearted sentiment about the Southerners that alike urged the support of the Confederacy. There was also a desire, on both humanitarian and practical grounds, to stop the war. But England wished to support the South without seeming to support slavery: this was difficult. While she wished to win the South for a friend, she did not want unnecessary trouble with the United States, then or later—although she did have it, then and later, despite her pains.★ But the Southerners were doing quite well. They could be gained as an ally later, since the need was mutual. Meanwhile, as long as prodigious profits were being made and Lancashire was quiet, there was no reason to hasten action unduly. At any moment, to be sure, a reason, at home or abroad, might emerge; but until it did... Very probably the Ministry reasoned that recognition was inevitable, but, if they waited for exactly the right moment, it would be quite clear to all—to the abolitionist groups, to the profit-making business men, even to the United States—that they really had no choice. The right moment came in the early autumn of 1862, and

★ The United States long remained hostile because of English support of the Confederacy (while that conquered land was bitter at the want of support). Moreover, the United States truculently claimed hundreds of millions of pounds for damage done by the CSS *Alabama*—both direct (ship sinkings) and indirect (prolonging the war by two years). After years of ill-tempered negotiations, England in 1872 paid fifteen million dollars on the less-fantastic claims. There is, when one recalls the gleeful cheers in the House and the pride of the vessel's builder, a certain irony in the then quite inconceivable aftermath.

Gladstone and Russell saw it; Palmerston did not. He wished to wait, past the moment of equilibrium, for a great Confederate victory on Northern soil, not as an assurance of ultimate success—which was beyond assurance sure—but as a manifestation of Confederate offensive strength to deter the United States from any thoughts of a Canadian adventure which would bring England into the field with the South. Gladstone and Russell were right and Palmerston was wrong, but he prevailed quite easily because they, too, probably thought that an even better moment would come. And in that thought lies the fundamental reason for England's inaction: the glittering illusion that without the lifting of an English hand the independence of the Confederate States was utterly certain.

The Glittering Illusion

The whole case against the 'Model Republic' was contained in the charge of precarious instability. By its very nature, a large democracy could not hold together. The profoundest student of American democracy, de Tocqueville, had thought that its continuance as one nation could "only be a fortunate accident."[4] But if the inexorable forces contained in its own being must divide it, then, clearly, when that inevitable break-up took place, not all the President's men could put it together again. The secession of the Southern states proved beyond question what had not indeed been questioned except by a few: the operation of this ineluctable law. And what could be more certain than that the men who had been unable to *prevent* the working of the law could not *reverse* its direction when the damage had been done? The law was proved by secession; its operation could no more be interrupted by Lincoln than a tidal wave by a king. This doctrine, after two nations stood where one had been, was accepted as men accept the relentless wheel of the planets.

Nothing further was needed, but there in fact existed

simultaneously a strong conviction based on history that, given certain conditions, revolutions could not fail. So it had been proved in countless cases: the Netherlands, Italy, the Spanish Colonies, and, above all, the Thirteen.★ The South more than met the conditions, namely, numerous revolutionaries in control of a large area; for the South had millions of unified and determined people controlling millions of square miles of territory, with able leaders and an organized government to boot. It could not, therefore, be conquered. "Does not every sane man believe it to be an impossibility"—said an M.P. in the course of a debate—"that the South can be over-mastered and put down?"[5]

The two immutable laws—one operating chiefly to foredoom Northern efforts, the other to predestine Southern independence—carried utter conviction to virtually everyone who could comprehend them, including partisans of the North.★★ Nothing that the North could do—unless it were to inspire the dreaded and terrible servile insurrection—and nothing that England could do or fail to do could alter the fact that the old Union was permanently divided. Moreover, the operation of the laws was further proved in the most simple and direct way possible: Northern armies again and again were defeated and driven out of Virginia. From Manassas (Bull Run) in 1861 to Gettysburg and Vicksburg on the same July day of 1863, the Confederacy won steadily and brilliantly. In the long run it is possible that the most important effect of these victories was not in North America, where they did not avert the conquest of the South, but in England, where they made it impossible for most Englishmen to entertain even the possibility of Northern victory. Even the Englishmen who urged, in speeches and in writing, the

★ It was forgotten how often foreign help—above all, to the Thirteen—had been decisive. And the power of steam was not understood.

★★ It was ironical that so many of the simple folk who could not comprehend the laws—or that the U.S. were not fighting to free the slaves—should have been justified both by U.S. victory & emancipation.

recognition of the South were thinking of cementing friendship and alliance with the Confederacy—*not* of saving it. The very admiration of England for the South in arms, for Lee and Jackson and Stuart, strengthened the conviction that they could never be defeated. Because this conviction, based on the 'laws' and on the chain of Southern victories, was so unalterable by 1863, Gettysburg was seen as only a regrettable but quite temporary check. And after Gettysburg the confirmed English nation continued to see only crafty withdrawal in retreats, major victories in minor ones, and missed altogether the ominous Northern constrictor slowly strangling the South. *The Confederacy was not seen to be losing until Sherman burned his savage way to the sea.* The day after that news arrived was 1865; and the Confederacy was collapsing too swiftly to stay or succour. "Almost to the very hour when the South, its brave and brilliant defense all over, had to yield...to the conquerors, the London public were still invited to believe that Mr. Davis was floating on the full flood of success."[6]

Thus, throughout the war to the very eve of Southern collapse, there was scarcely the shadow of a doubt that the old United States were permanently broken. Captain Chesney's study of the campaigns in Virginia not only suggested the impossibility of such armies as the Northern beating such armies as the Southern but gave facts to demonstrate that the South could resist indefinitely. Lord Stanley, writing to Disraeli on 15th July 1862 in connexion with a prospective meeting of top Conservatives to discuss the war, urged that mediation was useless and premature; by waiting until the next session, "when years of military and political failure will have justified President Lincoln to abandoning a hopeless undertaking", the chance of mediation's being accepted would be increased. In the same letter he suggests: "If we want to protract the war—to stimulate the combatants to the utmost, let us talk of interfering to stop it. If we want it to die out, let us carefully stand aloof."[7] Because, of course, the North must realize that it cannot conquer the South. Lord Stanley was concerned to stop the war, not to help

the North; but one may see his conviction that the United States
were engaged in a "hopeless undertaking" and that they might
realize its hopelessness sooner if England did not interfere. Indeed,
the English conviction of the impossibility of restoring the Union
was so sure, so profound, that Englishmen found it difficult to
understand why the United States failed to see what was so clear.
There was a general expectation that the North would see it quite
soon and give over the vain endeavour.

The most important source of news and attitudes in England—
one of the most powerful forces in all Europe, indeed—was *The
Times*. Innumerable other papers followed its judgments and its
opinions. We should note here that Gettysburg was July 1863; in
1864 Atlanta fell on September 2, and Sherman occupied Savan-
nah December 21 (the news reaching England on the last day of
the year, 1864). And yet *The Times,* confirming the opinion it
reflected, published such comments as the following:—

> [1861] the certain failure of all attempts at coercion — The
> reduction of the seceding States is an almost inconceivable idea
> — No war of independence ever terminated unsuccessfully ex-
> cept where the disparity of force is far greater than it is in this
> case —
> [1862] the odds [are] all on the Southern side — How long is
> this to last? Not long enough for the conquest of the South
> — [talk of] putting down and crushing out rebellion, is mere
> verbiage —
> [1863] sooner or later the North must see that its enterprise
> is hopeless, and that it must submit — They might as well try
> to save it [the Union] as the Heptarchy — they will just an-
> nihilate one another — as reunion is impossible — we suppose
> this terrible and cruel struggle will linger on till the North has
> no means left to fight — It will be found as impossible to over-
> whelm the native levies of men of English race fighting for their
> lives and possessions...as it was for Carthage...to break down
> the stubborn spirit of the less ably led Roman militia — sub-

jugation of the South [is] impossible —
[1864] The present prospects of the Confederates in this fourth
year of the war are brighter than ever before — The failure
of George III. was not more complete — The North must see
that it is persisting in an enterprise allowed by all Europe to
be hopeless, and proved to be so by events — We [have always]
said that the North could never subdue the South —
[October] Ruin stares the Union in the face —
[December] To negotiation it must come at last —
[1865] So long as that idol [the Union] stands on its pedestal
the war must rage on, and we see no prospect of its early ter-
mination—[March (just before the fall of Richmond)] if the
South shall resolve to stand out to the end, they [the U.S.] have
made but little progress towards the conclusion of the war — [8]

Thus the 'Thunderer', the most powerful and respected newspaper
in the world.

But this is not to blame *The Times* or to convict it of false prophecy: *The Times* and all England were in the grip of the glittering
illusion, that Jefferson Davis *had made* a nation. Without England's
having to risk a single warship, the end—desired as well as
expected—of the disintegration of the American colossus and the
establishment of a potential ally was virtually a *fait accompli.* Why
should *The Times* question what all history proved? And, of course,
any reports from America tending to suggest that the Confederates
were being defeated had got to be interpreted in the light of the
established fact that the Confederates *could not* be defeated. Furthermore, whatever the Yankees, well known to be liars, might say,
the Southerners—who, after all, ought to know—gave constant
assurances that they were not being and could not be conquered.
They rather pointedly refrained from asking for assistance; only
recognition.★ The Confederate Commissioner and all the high-

★ A wartime poem by John R. Thompson, apparently published in a Richmond,
Virginia, newspaper, reproaches England at length for not giving "with hearty
shake, the hand of nationality" (i.e., recognition); and it ends by saying that
"we" (Southerners) are "Convinced that we shall fairly win at last our nationality, / Without the help of Britain's arm, in spite of her neutrality."

ranking Southerners who moved among the English country houses repeated these assurances with calm and dignified force. The Confederate clergymen in their solemn protest against emancipation affirmed that Lincoln's objectives were unobtainable. The Union supporters in England were, for the most part, as convinced as their Confederate counterparts. "I believed as fully as anyone," said Goldwin Smith in 1865 to an audience in Boston, Massachusetts, "that the task which you had undertaken was hopeless, and... wished with all my heart that you would save the Border States, if you could, and let the rest go. Numbers of Englishmen—Englishmen of all classes and parties—who thought as I did at the outset, remain rooted in this opinion. They still [in 1865] sincerely believe that this is a hopeless war".[9] Just as writers who urged help for the South often felt obliged to point out that this implied no love of slavery on their part, so writers who favoured no-recognition or no-interference often felt obliged to point out that this implied no doubt of ultimate Confederate independence. Otherwise they might have been dismissed as too unrealistic to be heard. Indeed, the conviction was all but unanimous and, in general, it was the more thoughtful and historically minded (for instance, the historian Freeman) who were most deeply convinced. Just as, with a few notable exceptions, only the very simple, who believed that the war was a holy crusade of abolitionist Righteousness against slaveholding Wickedness and were impervious to any fact to the contrary, believed in Northern victory. It was more a faith than a belief, mocked by the more intelligent, and astonishingly vindicated. But the greater part of England, confident of their comprehension of the principles governing revolution and democracy, remained certain of Northern failure to the end. In a book on the cotton famine a letter, written in January 1865, says that England might as well "give up all hopes of American cotton till the North either finds by practical demonstration that they are defeated, or that their efforts have ended in a financial collapse."[10] Further illustrations of the illusion might be paraded literally by the hundred, but it seems unnecessary: *The Times* alone establishes its existence. In the newspapers and other journals, in books and pamphlets, in speeches and letters, sounds always the note of finality:[11]—

> Secession is accomplished—final and irrevocable—all historical precedents prove—everyone knows—no sane man doubts—they will never return—cannot be conquered—might be depopulated but cannot be forced back—reunion is impossible—they will never return—cannot be conquered—independence is absolutely sure—the North are spending millions all in a vain hope—the wildest optimist will not now deny a *fait accompli*—Lee will take Washington—they will never go back—there is no need for us to interfere at present—they will never return—never.

The glittering illusion.

And the result of this illusion was: "There is no need for us to interfere at present." *There is no need*—no urgency, no imperative. In a book entitled *The Second War of Independence in America,* published in London in 1863, the author wrote: "The Confederate States exhibit the picture of a well-organized Government, which exists not only de jure, as we have tried to show, but also de facto. No intervention of the European Powers is desired by this Government to secure its permanence. It is strong enough to maintain its independence unassisted."[12]

There are few writers on the War of Secession who have not remarked in passing this assurance of Southern success—and they have gone on to attribute England's failure to act to causes ranging from emergent democracy to a rather uncharacteristic timidity. But to propose the illusion as the cause of inaction—the essential underlying cause—is not to deny that there existed a multitude of reasons to avoid or delay action. But without the illusion—the illusion of Confederate independence already secured, of the United States permanently broken, of time in plenty—all of these reasons together could not, very probably, have withstood the tremendous pressure of the host of reasons urging action. To return to our original figure of the torrent and the dam: the reasons for inaction that we have examined—democracy, abolitionism, war profits, fear, and the rest—were the dam; against it swept the torrent—sympathy for the South, hatred of the North and fear of democracy, the desire to see the colossus broken, the hope of economic alliance and free trade with the South, and more. With the events of the war, the torrent became ever stronger, the dam weaker. It seemed to almost every contemporary only a matter of time until the dam broke—hence, the reaction to the Newcastle speech: "[The Government] have only followed the lead of the people, and followed it at far distance...The Cabinet is not to blame if...it obeys the national will."[13] Whether they were glad or regretful, Englishmen were not astonished: the dam had broken just as they had expected. But besides the torrent and the dam, there was a third and unknown element: the floodgate that was the illusion. Its effect was precisely to reduce all pressure. All that was to be gained by Southern independence was, in fact, gained already: the South will never come back, never. "No intervention...is desired by this Government... It is strong enough to maintain its independence unassisted." Justice and sympathy might prompt recognition and gestures of help, but not because either was necessary; the Southerners were no pathetic little band of revolutionaries about to be crushed by a great empire; they were about to march on Washington. Thus, though England wished to make the gesture of sympathy, and *would* make it in due course, there was no compelling reason to act at any given moment if other reasons for delay could be brought forward—as, of course, they always could be. Thus in 1862, when Lord Palmerston hesitated, Russell and Gladstone yielded. Thus Napoleon's proposals of joint action were rejected. England intended to act eventually; Englishmen of all parties expected action tomorrow or next week. But always it was not the right moment, not the perfect moment. There were excellent reasons not to act today. If the cotton lords and the cotton operatives were quiet; if business men were making great profits; if the Yankee mercantile marine was going to the bottom—then wait a little longer: Confederate independence is established. If Canada and the English mercantile marine might be endangered, if France was not quite to be trusted and it was not altogether desirable to have her in Mexico, if the Queen was nervous of war—then wait a little longer: the Southerners could not be conquered. Any of these reasons for delay might change soon and recognition become possible; but the brave South's freedom was *won*—and there was no hurry, no urgency.

England, after all, did not 'fail to act'. The question—*Shall England act or let the Confederacy go down?*—was *never* put. It was, rather: Must England offer recognition *now* if she would win the South for a friend? Must England intervene *now* to prevent revolution in Lancashire? And the answer was: No, not yet. The great issues were already won and were not in question: democracy had had the fatal stroke; the free-trading Confederacy was established; the American colossus was divided; the principle of freedom of nationalities was vindicated. As for the lesser things, Lancashire was doing without cotton very nicely so far; justice could be done to the South and the friendship established sometime soon, but not yet—anytime, as long as it is before the United States admit their failure and sue for peace. It was, in fact, never a question of *whether* but one of *when*. And the answer, invariably, was: not yet. Business men were not so greedy for gain as to prefer short-term to long-range profits: but if they could have both? The Government were not so fearful as to be incapable of venturing for a great stake: but if they could win the stake without risk? The governing classes were not at all blind to what was at issue: they merely thought the issue decided. Thus is explained the loyalty and discipline of a proud and intensely pro-Southern Parliament: they were quite willing to leave the question of *when* to the Ministry, no question of *whether* being involved; and so cheerfully voted down the private member's motions on recognition. All that seems strange in the spectacle of a proud and intensely pro-Southern nation calmly failing

to act until the swift incredible defeat made it too late, is explained
by the 'glittering illusion'.

It can be offered only as an opinion: that England would have
intervened if convinced that by her doing so *and not otherwise* would
the Confederacy be established. Had she believed that the South
could fail, she would have seized upon the Seven Days or the Invasion of Maryland as the occasion for action—war if necessary. The
pressures upon the dam—the pressures in Parliament and the nation, the sense of urgency—would have been quite irresistible had
it not been for the comfortable illusion. Ironically, Confederate
diplomacy fostered the illusion in every way: one can only speculate
as to whether it would have made a difference, whether it could
have been believed, had James Mason said privately and at once:
"We shall hold out for two years or more; we shall win battles;
but in the end we shall be overwhelmed unless England helps us."
But Mason could not have said that, for he and the South were
also under the illusion. This doubly-grounded illusion must be one
of the most remarkable in all history. It is also one of the most con-
sequential, for because of it a nation lost its right to exist and
aristocracy was discarded.

[1] M. Beloff, *op.cit.,* pp 41, 47.

[2] *The Times, (History),* p 373.

[3] Cited in Chap V, Note 11

[4] De Tocqueville, p 268.

[5] *Hansard,* CLXVIII, 548 (Mr Whiteside—Debate of 18 July 1862).

[6] Justin McCarthy, v III, p 339.

[7] W.D. Jones, *op.cit.,* pp 31-32 (from the Disraeli Papers).

[8] L.S., *The "Times" on the American War,* pp 8-16.

[9] Goldwin Smith, *England and America,* p 17.

[10] M.J. McHaffie, *Was It a Cotton Famine?,* London, 1865, p 19.

[11] All are actually fragmentary quotations from contemporary pamphlets and so forth, most of the phrases recurring again and again.

[12] E.M. Hudson, p 135.

[13] *The Spectator,* cited earlier, Rhodes, v IV, p 340.

Epilogue

What Was Sought And Lost

The Southern nation with magnificent courage and devotion sought independence and, defeated, lost its right to exist; and aristocracy, both Southern and English, was doomed by the immense triumph of equalitarian democracy. The aristocracy ('the rule of the best') thus discredited was indeed aristocracy, but, more precisely, it was in both countries squirearchy in balance with limited democracy. It was immediately ruined in the South, more slowly in England.

The Southern cause was described by the friends of the South in England and by the Southerners themselves (see p. 71 f) as "the cause of freedom", by which was meant the struggle of an oppressed nationality for self-government. The Southerners saw clearly that control of the Federal Government by the North, which had occurred with the election of Lincoln, must lead to their oppression; and they proved their nationhood by fighting and dying for it. And yet, now that the South has been conquered and the conquerors' interpretation of the war is taught in the schools, it is said that it was the North that fought for freedom. After all, it freed the oppressed blacks, didn't it? And the North was the more democratic— and democracy means freedom, doesn't it? But the blacks were not fighting to be free—many of them, indeed, would have fought for their white men if they had been let—and thus were not an oppressed nationality. And the North, disclaiming any intention of freeing the slaves, fought to conquer the South and compel it into a rejected Union. Wars of conquest are *not* "the cause of freedom."

Lord Acton, lover of freedom, is known for his familiar words: "All power tends to corrupt; absolute power corrupts absolutely." And it was Lord Acton who broke his heart over Lee's surrender because he believed that Lee was fighting the battle of English, as well as Southern, *freedom*. How is it that this honest and intelligent gentleman, concerned all his life with freedom, could, in direct opposition to present-day popular American belief, hold that the *Southern* cause was "the cause of freedom"? The answer is that he saw and feared, as Alexis de Toqueville, the most brilliant of all observers of American democracy, did, *the tyranny of the majority* in an unlimited democracy. If limited monarchy is preferable to absolute monarchy, is it possible (though it sounds like heresy to suggest it)—is it *possible* that limited democracy is preferable to absolute democracy?

The states of the deep South dissolved their connection with the voluntary union of the United States with marked legality at the beginning of 1861. For a quarter of a year no one knew that there was to be a war. Then Lincoln (unauthorised by the Constitution) called for troops; and the upper South, led by Virginia, seceded. War was Lincoln's choice. The point is, Lincoln *could* have chosen to let the South go in peace on the grounds that just government depends on the consent of the governed, and the Southern states had withdrawn that consent. But, said the North, the *majority* do consent, since there are more people in the North. Even if most of the people in the South do not consent, we in the North are the majority of the whole nation. Thus the rights of a minority, although a minority of millions, mean nothing. This is precisely what de Toqueville warned against: the tyranny of the majority. And Lord Acton was deeply convinced that the principle of States Rights was the best limitation upon the tyranny of the majority that had ever been devised. Thus Lee *did* represent the cause of freedom, and Lord Acton broke his heart over Lee's surrender because the principle of States Rights was finally and for ever denied.

The America of today is the America that won that immense triumph in the war—the triumph of unlimited, equalitarian democracy. And its leaders have blurred the distinction between freedom and equality to the point where many people use those words as virtually interchangeable terms. 'Freedom from want' implying every man's equal right to food may be indeed a right but it is not freedom; it *is* his freedom, though, to take action to improve his needy state. What most people are unaware of is that freedom and equality, though revolutionaries may shout for both, are uneasy bedfellows and, in fact, often opposed, each tending to limit the other. Nearly every law designed to bring about greater equality, as so many of the laws of the late-twentieth century do intend, limits freedom. The freedom of the bright student to learn swiftly is limited by equalitarian schools for the average. Quotas in hiring limit the freedom of choice of the employer. Enforced admission of women or blacks to clubs and pubs limits freedom of association. Equality, not of opportunity but of rewards, is essentially a denial of quality—qualitative difference. A society that has a gentry of 'the quality' with their own schools, clubs, and preserves may be a free society but it will not be an equalitarian one. What won the war was equalitarian democracy.

The Southern nation, after a brief, intense, and heroic existence, was defeated, and then, as a conquered province, was subjected to the demeaning brutalities of 'Reconstruction' and subsequently to economic discrimination. The defeated Southerners, especially the women, would never forgive whilst their lives lasted. The English supporters of the South could sadly lay away their loves and hopes, but the Southerners, treated as villains in a ruined Southland, could not put continuing disaster out of mind. But their sons' sons, knowing the ante-bellum South and the Confederacy only as an old tale, taught in school the conquerors' interpretation of the causes of the war, were growing up *American*. It has happened to a thousand conquered lands in the surge and flow of empire: Gaul under the Romans, Celtic Britain under the Anglo-

Saxons, Anglo-Saxon England under the Normans. American values, like American industry and Interstates and, finally, TV, have penetrated the South; and American equalitarian democracy has been increasingly accepted as the norm, in England as well as the South. Matthew Arnold had asked (see p. 52) what influence might help to "prevent the English people from becoming, with the growth of democracy, *Americanised?*" But that unlimited, American, equalitarian democracy was what won in 1865. The Southerners in the late twentieth-century South might remain a bit sentimental about the song "Dixie" and put the Battle Flag on a license plate, but they had become too Americanised to know what was Southern and what was not. Indeed, in their hearts they supposed that it was for the better that the North—that *America*—had won.

If the Confederacy had won, the twentieth-century Southerners would of course hold that to have been for the better. But perhaps it really *is* for the better that America won. After all, the slaves *were* freed, and the forcibly Re-United States is big enough, powerful enough to stand up to the Russians and *their* conquests. The implied question—which would really be for the better?—cannot be answered, for it is not given us to know what might have lain along the road not taken. Moreover, we who would judge between the roads if both could be known are the people, both English and Southern, who have been shaped by what *did* win. We, therefore, suppose that unlimited equalitarian democracy is the very finest fruit of all the ages. Still, it may be said with some confidence that, had the Confederate States won their independence, the Southern slaves would almost certainly have been gradually emancipated. Before the war, Virginia had come within a few votes of freeing its slaves; and Robert E. Lee, like Jefferson, had freed his. Regardless of the victor, the 'peculiar institution' would be but a memory today. And, with respect to Russia, it is possible that three English nations on this continent—the USA, the CSA, and Canada—would be as formidable as two.

Still, how would an independent South that had freed its slaves be different? For one thing the plantation squirearchy would have survived, and democracy and aristocracy in the South would limit each other. Then, too, the former slaves while freed might not have been raised to full citizenship: in what Calhoun called a 'Greek democracy'—meaning that, like ancient Athens, its democracy rested upon slavery—there would not be the stress upon equality that marks the victorious America even if the slaves had ceased to be slaves. The South before the war had rejected industrialisation; perhaps it would have continued to reject it in favour of a greener, agrarian future. The unanswerable question is, how would that Southern squirearchy and the English squirearchy have evolved if unlimited, equalitarian democracy had, instead of achieving an enormous victory, been discredited (as many Englishmen thought it already had been through secession) by Southern victory, and had come to be seen as an unstable and dangerous form of government? One way that society might have evolved, a way often discussed in England, was a different sort of democracy or 'mixed constitution' in which the major *interests* in the commonwealth would be equally represented, regardless of numbers: that is, the rural squirearchy, the commercial middle class of the towns, the industrial workers, the rural yeomen or small farmers, and perhaps the professional men including the university dons. No interest, despite numbers, could dominate, nor could the city dominate the country; yet everybody would be represented within his order. It would be difficult to say that such a way would be less just than the modern system of the absolute majority. Another possiblity—a most intriguing one—for a *limited* democracy as opposed to an unlimited or absolute democracy is what we may call the Multiple-Vote society, an idea apparently originating with John Stuart Mill. Under this system everybody (even the emancipated slaves in the Confederacy) would have one vote by virtue of being alive, but, just as it is possible for one man to earn more than another, so it would be possible for the citizen to earn additional votes up to ten or fifteen. He might become a two-vote man by completing an upper school, and university graduates three. Other votes might be gained by service in the armed forces, by owning and ecologically caring for land, by distinction in one's occupation including arts and letters, or by valiant or distinguished service to the nation. Thus, while everyone would have a vote, ability—or quality—would have more weight at the polls; and it has been suggested that a much higher level of elected officials would result. It would be democracy but not equality of rewards, only of opportunity. But for either of these systems— representation of the great interests or the multiple vote—to have been seriously considered, the complete discrediting of American equalitarian democracy by victory of the South would have had to occur. Still, these are ways in which an independent Confederacy—and England—might have developed differently.

Reasons for calling the Southern cause the cause of freedom have been suggested, and equalitarianism has been singled out as the chief mark of the industrial, unlimited democracy that the United States was moving towards: "the tyranny of the majority" over minorities that de Toqueville warned against and Lord Acton feared—and the South suffered from. Of course all this is shocking democratic heresy, but it is so because unlimited, equalitarian democracy is what won, in England and the South as well as in 'America'. What men fight for, whether they know it or not, is what results from or would result from their victory. Let us pursue a little further what the Southern nation fought for.

What the South Fought For
Freedom v. Equality

The Thirteen Colonies in their War of Independence had fought for freedom. But the French Revolution (a true revolution of an underclass) proclaimed not only liberty but equality: and that idea was loosed upon the world. But liberty (freedom) and equality are natural allies only up to a point, and then enemies. They were opposed to a degree imperfectly understood by either side in the War of Southern Independence. Which principle was henceforth to limit the other? That question was at issue.

The North, fighting for a compelled union, won; but what also won was ever broadening equality, limiting freedom. More immediately what won was—America. Henceforth Virginians and Carolinians were to be Americans and even, with a grim irony, Yankees. 'The United States' ceased to be a plural term: a nation supplanted the united nations. Even the word 'Union' disappeared, for the ghost of the old, dead, voluntary union of states clung about it and made it unAmerican. The Negro also won the war, almost incidentally, for the North did not fight for him but against his master: it was not a crusade, except for a few; and emancipation, limited to the Confederacy, was an act of war, not humanity. But the great, hidden victory was that of equality: the very words 'freedom' and 'equality' became confused and virtually synonymous. Now, said Karl Marx in 1866, the United States are "entering the revolutionary phase."

What won the war everywhere was 'the people': equality not quality. Instead of two voices in balance, aristocracy and democracy, only one. Nothing henceforth was to be safe that did not have the sanction of the majority of the people, even nominally in Russia. Now the duke and the university don were to be admitted to equality with the docker; three dockers were superior to the duke and the don. Minorities ceased to have rights, despite constitutions, but only privilege sanctioned by the majority. The withdrawal of the Southern states was not sanctioned, though Virginia had entered the Union with the proviso that she could withdraw. The Mormons who trekked to remote Utah because of their religious belief in polygamy did not have that sanction, despite the Constitution. And from the majority there is no appeal.

Once it had been possible to appeal from lord to king and from king to Church. Perhaps such balance can exist only in the moment of transition from one unlimited power to another. In the United

States there was no such balance in reality, for President and even Supreme Court spoke in the name of the people (the Court 'interpreting' the Constitution in that name). It was in the name of the majority of the people (more people in the North) that Lincoln conquered the Confederacy. And it is quite immaterial whether the majority, in fact, want what is done in their name: they cannot resist themselves or appeal from themselves.

Lord Acton, lover of freedom and hater of the corruption of power, prophesied rightly that this sort of "spurious liberty" must affect the rest of the world, and went on to say: "By exhibiting the spectacle of a people claiming to be free, but whose love of freedom means hatred of inequality. . . and reliance on the State as an instrument to mould as well as control society, [the North] calls on its admirers to hate aristocracy and teaches its adversaries to fear the people."

Who could deny that America relies on the State as an instrument to mould society? In the early days of the Republic men criticized by their fellows were given to saying, "It's a free country, isn't it?" Who says it today? The states of the South were adversaries of the Northern majority: four years later they had learnt to fear the people. This is what won the war: the principle that three pawns take two castles and five pawns take the knights as well.

It is not enough to say that the South fought for slavery—although it *is* said. It is not enough to say that the South fought for free trade—although it *was* said. It is not even enough to say that the South fought for states rights. All three are true in a sense, but none tells us why the South fought and died. The South fought because it was invaded; indeed Virginia withdrew from the Union only because Lincoln intended invasion of the earlier seceded states. Then there were alien feet upon the soil of old Virginia—and in due course upon Georgia—and Southerners fought to defend what men hold dear, their homes and their land, not for conquest.

But the simple truth is that the South fought for freedom, the freedom to go their own way, the freedom to govern themselves.

They had exercised this freedom, but the North denied it and invaded. Two societies, two ways of life, clashed: *at issue was the compelled conformity of the smaller to the larger.* The difference between the two societies, which in colonial days had been between the dominance of 'God's elect' in Puritan New England and that of great landowners in Virginia and Carolina, was deepened by climate and distance, by immigration in the North and by slave-based squirearchy in the South, and became irreconcilable, except by war or separation, when the North began in the half-born age of steam its mutation into an industrial democracy and the South remained an agrarian aristocracy.

The Southern states were in form a democracy—a slave-based 'Greek democracy'—but equalitarian democracy in the South was in retreat to the hills: where the Planter came (wherever the great staples would grow) he brought the ideal of the landed estate and the chivalrous gentleman. To describe both Northerners and Southerners of that time as 'Americans' in today's usage is to do violence to the truth: they were alien as well as alienated. Slavery was the economic basis of Southern society, free trade was its interest, and state rights was its defence. It fought for a way of life based upon slavery, not for slavery—an essential distinction, for squirearchy could have been based upon serfdom or tenantry and have been fought for—and against—all the same. To say that the South's *cause*—freedom—was stained by slavery is to say that the cause of the Greeks at Marathon was stained by slavery. Both fought for freedom against invaders. Both would have given up their slaves for freedom, as the South privately offered to do for English help. The South had not yielded to the new condemnation of slavery; in time it undoubtedly would have done; but time was not permitted; and the alien morality of an alien majority was imposed by conquest.

The South rightly saw a menace to its way of life in the control of the federal government by the Northern majority, and withdrew from the Union. The remaining United States could have let the

Confederate States go in peace, as England was to let Canada and India go. But implicit in American democracy was the dogma that minorities—Southern or Mormon—must not be permitted to go their own way but must be compelled to conform to the will of the majority: 'the king can do no wrong.' For that reason, and no other, it was 'the irrepressible conflict.'—"If ever the free institutions of America are destroyed," said Alexis de Tocqueville in 1835, "that event may be attributed to the unlimited authority of the majority, which may at some future time urge the minorities to desperation, and oblige them to have recourse to physical force. ... [I]t will have been brought about by despotism [of the majority]."

The Southerners were, precisely, such a minority fighting that "unlimited authority." In Lord Acton's words, the Southerners "denied the justice of the doctrine that the minority possesses nothing which is exempt from the control of the majority," and the very invoking of the right of secession was "a distinct repudiation of the doctrine that the minority can enforce no rights, and the majority can commit no wrong." Secession, arguably implicit in the constitutional compact, was the counter to the absolutism of the (distant) majority. When the North refused to allow it, the appeal was to the sword, and the right of secession perished. Lord Acton wrote later: "I mourn for the stake which was lost at Richmond more deeply than I rejoice over that which was saved at Waterloo."

The South fought for the principles of 1776—the Declaration of Independence. The North, in flat denial of those principles, invaded a country whose nationhood was proved by a way of life men willingly defended and died to save. It was a way of life that was aristocratic and based (though not necessarily) upon slavery and that was (necessarily) opposed to conformity with Northern democracy. By the very nature of that democracy perhaps, it could not suffer its will to be spurned by letting the South go in peace. The South had no choice but to conform or fight for freedom. Like the Greeks confronted by the might of Persia, the South chose to fight against odds for freedom, loving freedom—again like the Greeks—not less because they held slaves. And that was the splendour they died for—the great name of freedom. But what came on, huge and very vindictive, armed with steam and endless guns, bearing the compulsive mandate of the majority of the 'whole people' (i.e., the North), was not to be withstood. The South had only its heartbreaking valour and General Lee. Four years it stood with desperate fortitude, praying for help from England, and then went down and was drowned.

The Thirteen Colonies in the First American War of Independence were far less unified, less organised, and less brilliantly led than the Confederate South. One estimate of Colonial sympathies has it that there were no more than roughly a third of the Colonials who were determined Patriots (revolutionaries) while another third were 'Tories' loyal to King and Empire. The rest, the last third, wished only not to be involved. It was France that made the decisive difference. France had little affection for English Colonials and less for revolutionaries, but she had a great desire to strike back at the England that had sunk her fleets and destroyed the French Empire in the New World; so she intervened with troops and ships; and the Colonies became independent. And France herself, having subsequently had her fleet sunk again, was hastened, by her expenditures in behalf of the Colonies, towards her own savage Revolution. But for France, the Thirteen Colonies would probably have been subdued by England. This would not necessarily have resulted in sore and resentful colonies, especially if England had been generous in victory. The Colonial Tories of course would have been delighted and the 'neutral' third not displeased. At all events, if English America (including Canada) had remained within the British Empire, the future history of that Empire and of the world might have been very different indeed. But France *did* intervene.

The Confederate South, despite vast territory and brilliant generals and valiant armies, lost the Second American War of Independence.

England, despite 'cotton hunger', despite her passionate sympathy for the Southerners, and despite all that she herself had at stake, "committed the unpardonable blunder, from her point of view, of not supporting the Southern States", as the German General von Bernhardi put it. And yet as the key man in making that "unpardonable blunder"—Lord Palmerston—said, a war in alliance with the Confederacy, supported by a willing France, against the remaining United States, would have been: "not perhaps a very formidable thing for England and France combined." But the "unpardonable blunder" was not Palmerston's alone. All England and the Southerners as well were making it, too, in their certainty that the South must inevitably win without English help: the glittering illusion.

And yet Lord Palmerston *was* the key man. What if he had been, precisely, *disillusioned*? Let us suppose a far-sighted and brilliant Englishman who was also a close and trusted friend of the Prime Minister: and then one evening round the fire at Number 10 Downing St, the port glowing in the lamplight, the friend convinces 'Pam' that the South must ineluctably be conquered with the resultant triumph of unlimited equalitarian democracy, and that the future of the world, not just America, lies in his lordship's hands. Palmerston is *convinced,* and Palmerston is not a timid man. He would, I believe, have acted at once. The moment is 1862, when Palmerston has already suggested that the time for action is perhaps at hand, with the firm agreement of Russell and Gladstone—the Triumvirate. The rest of the Cabinet would have gone along. And Parliament would have gone along with cheers. First, perhaps, an offer of mediation, spurned as expected by the United States. Then recognition of the Confederate States of America. And then, in the end, intervention. It could so easily have happened had Lord Palmerston been convinced that otherwise the South would be conquered. What would have been the result? What would the world look like if 'the Allies' had established Southern independence?

It can only be speculation along the lines of the probable. Still, let us speculate. Let us suppose merely that clear-sighted friend of

Lord Palmerston—the key to the key, so to speak—and the timely conviction of his lordship. Let us endeavour to see by a bit of 'whatifery' what the English friends of the South were really fighting for on the lecture platform and with the pen. What did they hope for? What would have happened if England had *not* committed "the unpardonable blunder"? Let us imagine what would have followed Allied victory, both immediately and in the remoter future of the twentieth century if the Confederate armies had been supported by the power of Great Britain and the Royal Navy.

In the following sketch, Part I is a brief recapitulation of the situation in England at that moment when the Triumvirate were, in fact, *almost* in agreement that the time for action had come, and England expected ministerial action momently. And Part II is what was *then* the probable. All the quotations are genuine, except that those in Part II are skewed out of context. (See Chapter V for the proper contexts.) The quotations from Sir Winston Churchill are from his own bit of whatifery, "If Lee Had Not Won the Battle of Gettysburg" in *If It Had Happened Otherwise* (Ed., J.C. Squires, London, 1931).

The sketch, we must imagine, is written by a British historian of our day, writing in the cloistered quiet of All Souls College in Oxford, Oxford the home of lost causes. But here the Lost Cause had not been lost but won. And the world of *today,* therefore, is not the world we know.

After The South Won

Richmond Enquirer

VOL. XXV	JULY 4, 1863	NO. 5

LEE WINS AT GETTYSBURG
WASHINGTON FALLS
NORTH SUES FOR PEACE

Part One: The Historical Position in 1862

In that year the balance of the bayonets on the battlefields of North America was plainly falling on the Southern side, owing to the genius of General Lee. In England, watching with the absorbed attention that had never waned after *The Times'* vivid account of the battle near Washington at Manassas and the passions aroused by the *Trent* affair, everyone knew that English recognition of the Confederate States and even intervention were more than a possibility.

Many of the 'educated million,' deeply sympathetic to the South, expected action by the Government at any moment. Powerful men, who believed that the traditional English way of life would be endangered by a Northern success, endeavoured to force the Cabinet to ensure Confederate independence. Others, deeply stirred by the valiant struggle of the South, urged England to help it as they had helped freedom fighters in Greece and Italy. Countless appeals stressed the same points: The South is English, unlike the North which has become mongrel through immigration. Moreover, the

South is led by gentlemen—English gentlemen—and the war is (as one columnist summed up the general sentiment) an affair of 'Gentlemen v. Cads.' The Southerners, our kinsmen, have proved by their indomitable spirit that they are worthy of independence; England must abide her traditions and help them.

A.J.B. Beresford Hope, the brother-in-law of the Marquess of Salisbury, wrote: "I declare that the cause of the South is the cause of freedom, the cause of those principles of constitutional government which we desire to see prevailing all over the world...If we made allowances for Italy, should we not be willing to make equal allowances for our own flesh and blood...who are tying to raise up a new English nation...? They have passed the Red Sea—shall we never give them a hand that they may reach the promised land?" Such an appeal, it would seem, could not be made in vain. Indeed, that keen French observer of the English scene, Louis Blanc, wrote for his paper in France early in 1862: "I say...without hesitation, because I think it to be a fact, that everything here [in England] is preparing for a signal recognition of the Southern States." Thus when Gladstone, one of 'the Triumvirate' that led the Cabinet, told the wildly cheering crown at Newcastle that Jefferson Davis had made, not only an Army and a Navy but a *Nation*, it was held to be tantamount to Recognition. As the pro-Northern *Spectator* said: "We cannot...blame the Cabinet. They have only followed the lead of the people, and followed it at far distance. The educated million in England, with here and there an exception, have become unmistakably Southern...[T]he Cabinet has made up its mind that the American struggle is over, and that henceforward two nations must exist on the American continent." Far from disagreeing with *The Spectator*, Louis Blanc was inclined to suspect that Gladstone was "courting popularity" by appealing to the universal Southern feeling; Gladstone's words, he said, "went straight to the heart of the nation," which responded with a great cry of "Down with the North! The South for ever!" All England awaited the next move.

Part Two: The Then-Probable

All England awaited the next move. There was not long to wait. The Cabinet, after, in Lord Acton's words, "taking one of the most momentous resolutions ever adopted by a Ministry," were now prepared to move swiftly. The Newcastle speech was delivered on October 7th, 1862, and on the first day of November England and France, which had long advocated such a joint move, proposed mediation to the warring American nations. It was a favourable moment, for, as Gladstone had observed in his Memorandum to the Cabinet, "fortunes have been placed for the moment *in equilibrio* by the failure of the main invasions on both sides." That the Confederate States would gratefully accept the good offices of the European powers and the United States belligerently refuse them had been expected by the Ministry. Both the acceptance and the rejection were by the 25th of November in the hands of Lord John Russell, the Foreign Secretary. But, as he himself had said earlier, if the North refused mediation, England would have no alternative but to recognise the South. On the first day of December, therefore, the Queen's Proclamation recognising the Confederate States of America was issued, to be followed by that of France and other powers. It was at this juncture there occurred the famous dialogue between the Foreign Secretary and the United States Minister in which his lordship endeared himself to generations of schoolboys by uttering what has become, by reason of its brevity, his most memorable remark. Making his final call before sailing, Minister Adams said stiffly: "It would be superfluous in me to point out to your Lordship that this is war." Rising to show that the interview was over, his lordship said: "Damme! Quite!"

The events which followed are familiar to everyone. The welcome tidings of their recognition reached the Confederate States on December 12th, and on the following day Lee's army, no doubt heartened by the news, crushed the enemy at Fredericksburg. Nevertheless, the United States, refusing even in defeat to accept what all the world could see must be accepted, declared war—with a courage that was as admirable as it was foolish—on both England and France. It was regrettable but, as Lord Palmerston, the Prime Minister, said, "not perhaps a very formidable thing for England and France combined."

And the editor of *The Times* wrote to Russell that "the whole Army, Navy and Volunteers are of one mind and all mad for service in America. For once, the Navy has been found ready when wanted; as to the Army, we might recruit each company into a battalion if necessary." The Government, though, intended to leave the operations on land in the capable hands of the Confederates, merely reinforcing the troops in Canada. But there was work for the Navy. As Winston Churchill observed in his study of this war, "The Northern blockade could not be maintained even for a day in the face of the immense naval power of Britain", and, as he also wrote, "The Northern forces at New Orleans were themselves immediately cut off and forced to capitulate." This event caused huge celebrations in London, less because an old defeat was thus avenged than because of the summary hanging of General "Beast" Butler from the yardarm of the Royal Navy flagship.

We need not linger over the subsequent events of the war. Despite another grave defeat at Chancellorsville in the spring of 1863 and a growing peace party in the North, the United States continued to resist and even to make preparations to send an expedition into Canada. The Cabinet, therefore, decided to avert such an invasion, if possible, by reinforcing the Confederate armies. Two months later General Lee led his veteran army across the United States frontier into Pennsylvania, and the British Expeditionary Force, which had just been landed in Virginia, were sent after him. Before they reached the scene, Lee had joined battle with a large American army near the village of Gettysburg.

Winston S. Churchill, in his thoughtful study, "If Lee Had Not Won the Battle of Gettysburg," has shown how close an affair it really was. The crucial moment came on the third day when Lee ordered an attack on the strong Northern centre. Pickett and the Virginians swept forward into their deathless charge. But, gallant as it was, we know now that the Union fire would almost certainly have so cut down the Virginians that they would have been unable to hold the position if they had gained it. But in one of those time- ly arrivals that suggest the workings of Providence, the British brigades, having been apprised of the tactical disposition by units of Stuart's cavalry, were, just at the moment of the launching of Pickett's charge, driving into the Union rear, led by the Coldstream Guards. The resulting panic of the entire Union left as the English and the Virginians joined hands, cutting the U.S. army into two, led to Meade's surrender. The field was won—and the war as well. The formal surrender was on the fourth of July—Confederate In- dependence Day—even as Stuart was riding into Washington. Three days later, the Allies entered Washington unopposed. And a fort- night later the United States Government at the new Capital in Portland, Maine, yielded to the universal cry for peace and capitulated.

It is not necessary to examine the generous terms of peace that the Allies imposed. Our concern is rather with the effects of the victory on the Allies themselves. The Confederacy was now indepen- dent, and England had now a firm friend in the new world. As Chur- chill put it, "Gladstone achieved not merely the recognition but an abiding alliance between Great Britain and the Southern States." It was an alliance destined to become even closer when the South became, somewhat later, a member of the British Commonwealth, and its President became Prime Minister, with a Royal Governor to open the Parliament at Richmond in the name of the Queen.

In England one of the first effects of the victory was that John Bright and indeed the "Manchester School" lost such influence as they possessed. It was widely recognised that they had supported the brutal attempt of the United States to conquer the Confederacy in hopes of gaining power through the working classes. But these had not been much impressed; the great heart of England was sound in this struggle between Northern conquest and Southern freedom. One historian has, we may notice, suggested that the failure of the working classes to raise a cry for Government action in the great cotton famine might be interpreted as sympathy for the North or for the doctrines of John Bright; but the fact that in Liverpool—the most Confederate city outside the Confederacy—no sympathizer with the United States could even hold a job, tells against the interpretation. It is surely far more probable, as most historians agree, that their quiet was simply the proverbial patience of the British working man and his trust in the Queen's Government—which, as the event demonstrated, was very well founded indeed.

The decline of the 'Manchester School' was but a sign of the underlying reality of the discrediting of the doctrine they had preached: the universal suffrage that must lead to that tyranny of the majority de Tocqueville had warned against and the Southern States had suffered from. The general recognition that it was a dangerously unsound doctrine was decisively shown in England by the overwhelming failure of the Reform Bill of 1867. We today who perceive the fatal flaw, the lack of balance, in the doctrine that three dockers should outweigh the duke and the don—that, so to speak, the pawns should take the knights and the castles—may wonder how some Englishmen in the 1860s could even have considered it; but it must be remembered that the United States before the War of Northern Aggression had held forth a beguiling if specious promise of prosperity as well as proclaiming a spurious 'liberty' that was, in fact, not liberty but equality. And our present concept of a balanced society in which the major elements—the business interest, the working classes of the cities, and the rural people—are equally represented, regardless of numbers, which may be called true equality, and each with that veto upon the others that is so sure a protection to minorities: such a concept was then scarcely a dream.

It must indeed be regarded as one of the fruits of that great victory upon the plains of Pennsylvania, a victory now regarded as the most decisive since Waterloo. Some, in fact, believe it to be *more* important: Lord Acton, more aware than most people of the corruption of power, including that of the majority, said that he rejoiced more deeply over the stake won by the South at Gettysburg than that saved at Waterloo.

Another result of that victory has been the firm establishment of the principle of self-determination, to which even the United States and Russia now give assent. An equally important result of the victory was, as the Confederate Commissioner to London, J.M. Mason—Sir James as he became—had promised, the gradual ending of slavery. It was in 1875 that the Southern Prime Minister, Lord Arlington—or, to use a more familiar designation, General Lee—announced that the several states had agreed that all slaves born after the last day of 1879 would be free; and the Confederacy thereupon embarked on the benign programme of slowly raising the Negro to the limits of his ability. A few years later the United States also emancipated the small number of slaves in their territories. We can only be grateful that emancipation of the slaves in the South came about in this way and that the sinister Emancipation Proclamation of President Lincoln—an invitation to the slaves to rise against their masters, or more precisely their mistresses, since the men were with the army—had no effect. Lincoln, himself, an inherently kindly man, has confessed in his *Apology for My Administration* (Portland, 1871) that he was deeply thankful that the slaves did not rise.

One more result of the Allied victory at Gettysburg must not be neglected: the complete discrediting of that barbarism in warfare that marked the efforts of the Americans to subdue the Southerners—the barbarism of Generals Sherman and Sheridan and "Beast" Butler. It is to be hoped that no civilised nation will again make use of such methods. There is, indeed, reason to hope that no civilised nation will again resort to war of any sort. In the seventy-five years of world peace which have followed the Great War or One Year War of 1914-1915 when the Allies so completely defeated Germany—a victory, incidentally, that might not have been so swiftly won but for the Confederate divisions under the second Marquess of Arlington—the Kaisers appear to have relinquished their dreams of militaristic glory.

These then, are some of the things that such far-sighted Englishmen as Beresford Hope and the many other supporters of the South fought for on the lecture platform and with the pen, while General Lee and the Army of Northern Virginia fought so gallantly in the field. The world owes them a great deal. Had these dedicated English supporters of the South not perceived what was at issue, England might not have acted; and there is a real possiblity—though many historians will disagree—that if England had remained neutral, the United States with their vast resources might have conquered the South and occupied it as an inferior province. All in all, they had a remarkably clear vision of what was at stake. And these things were at issue when Lord Palmerston's Ministry took their most momentous decision. They were at issue when, in Winston Churchill's resounding words, the Allies "by a deathless feat of arms broke the Union front at Gettysburg and laid open a fair future to the world."

Appendix

The British Dominion of the South

Never perhaps in the history of the British Empire was that Empire less valued than it was in the sixties. That was the South's misfortune, for she appears to have hinted, in rather a delicate and lady-like manner, that she regretted her hastiness in 1776 and, after all, preferred Old England to New England. If pressed with suitable inducements, she might be willing to renew the formal bond. Such a hint might well have fallen upon receptive ears in England, not only in the eighteenth century but also one or two decades later in the nineteenth. She might then have been regarded as worth fighting for. Had England intervened and the South resumed the Imperial tie, in due course joining Australia and Canada and the others in the Commonwealth, the whole of subsequent English (and European) history might have been different: for instance, in 1914. It may not be worth the speculation for its own sake, but the history of English sympathy for the Southern Confederacy—a passionate sympathy that did not greatly affect history—is not complete without reference to this small intriguing current, although it too came to nothing. There can hardly be doubt that, if that were her price for intervention, England could have recovered half her lost colonies as well as rather more—including Texas... The following quotations which bear on this subject are given without further comment. There were, doubtless, many more on both sides of the Atlantic.—

[c. 1851] Carlyle, who had written a Latter Day Pamphlet on the Negro question and who believed in superior races, "received from eminent Southerners letters suggesting that England should restore slavery in her West Indian possessions, in which case the slave States would unite with them, and a great British empire be formed in the New World. . . . It did startle me that eminent Southerners, some ten years before the war, should have wished to throw their States and slavery under the protection of the British flag". [M.D. Conway, *Autobiography,* 2 vol, London, 1904, v I, p 365.

[1860] The British Consul at Charleston, South Carolina, wrote to the British Minister at Washington an account of a dinner at the Jockey Club—composed of the 'best people', the 'gentlemanly interest'—where he had referred to the prizes of the Turf and the Plates run for the various colonies, adding: "'I cannot help calling your attention to the great loss you yourselves have suffered by ceasing to be a Colonial Dependency of Great Britain, and I am sure that if you had continued to be so, the Queen would have had great pleasure in sending you some Plates too'. Of course this was meant for the broadest sort of joke, calculated to raise a laugh after dinner, but to my amazement, the company chose to take me literally, and applauded for about ten minutes—in fact I could not go on for some time." [E.D. Adams, *Great Britain & the American Civil War,* 2 vol., London, 1925, v I, p 43.]

[1860] Judah P. Benjamin of Louisiana, later C.S. Secretary of State (and still later member of the English bar), wrote to the British Consul at New York on a matter of the "greatest importance and interest to Her Britannic Majesty's kingdom". After speaking of the almost certain election of the Republican candidate and the resultant destruction of all plantation interests, he wrote that this "the South, as sure as there is a God in Heaven, will not submit to. Sooner than yield. . . we will. . . upon certain conditions, *at once return to our allegiance to Great Britain, our Mother Country.* Many, very many, of the most wealthy and influential planters throughout the South have already discussed this alternative, in the event of the election of Mr. Lincoln, and the popularity of the proposition seems to pass from one to another almost with an elastic rapidity. It is true they have made no public demonstration of their intentions, for such a course would be attended with direful consequences at this time, *but the Pear will be fully ripe before November.* Gossiping newsmongers and babbling pothouse politicians are not allowed to know what is going on in their very midst. Select dinner parties come off every day throughout the whole South, and not one of them ends without a strong accession to our forces. I have even heard some of them address each other by titles already. My chief object in approaching you is to cultivate your friendship, and procure your coöperation in aid of accomplishing this grand object of returning to the dominion of our fathers' Kingdom.'' Benjamin then discusses his intention of approaching Lord Lyons at Washington, and concludes by saying that the Consul's assistance in this great affair will win him the reward of the Queen and a ''hearty cheer from every true Briton's heart for having aided in the return of the National Prodigals.'' (See Note below also.) [T. Weed & others, *The Life of Thurlow Weed,* 2 vol., Boston, 1883-84, v II, pp 313-14.]

Note: When the above Life was published in 1884, Benjamin—then engaged in his third, or English, career—denied authorship of the letter, although saying that ''The letter is...to some extent founded on fact.'' He also said that when asked by Englishmen of high position if the South might not be better off with a monarch, he ''said on many occasions to persons who I thought would advantageously echo my words that the best thing that could happen to the Southerns would be for Queen Victoria to make them a present of her second son and place her third son over Canada.'' Benjamin thought the letter in question was written by a Southern Congressman, which is probable—*if* he did not in fact write it. [Quotations from R.D. Meade, *Judah P. Benjamin,* N.Y., 1943, pp 140-141.]

[1861] "Mr. Edmund Rhett, one of the active and influential political family of that name,...a very intelligent and agreeable gentleman,...declared there were few persons in South Carolina who would not sooner ask great [sic] Britain to take back the State than submit to the triumph of the Yankees." [W.H. Russell, *My Diary North & South,* 2 vol., London, 1863, v I, p 214.]

[1861] "W.H. Russell, correspondent of the *Times,* reported in the spring, 1861, that he frequently heard the same sentiment in the South. 'Then cropped out again the expression of regret for the rebellion of 1776, and the desire that if it came to the worst, England would receive back her erring children, or give them a prince under whom they could secure a monarchial form of government. There is no doubt about the earnestness with which these things are said.' Russell's *Diary* is largely a condensation of his letters to the *Times.* In the letter of April 30, 1861 (published May 28), he dilates to the extent of a column on the yearning of South Carolina for a restoration of colonial relations." [E.D. Adams, *op.cit,* v I, p 54 & fn.]

[1861] Leader in *The Times:* "We have been told, in fact,...by Southern leaders that they are half inclined to become British once more. Both sides are bidding for us". [E.D. Adams, *op.cit.,* v I, p 97.]

[1862] An Englishman, in a pamphlet of 1862, speaks of John Caldwell Calhoun whom he apparently knew quite well: "I was myself present in 1839 when the leader of the South urged an English gentleman to allow himself to be commissioned by the South to bring before the English Government the position of the South, for the purpose of assuring it that the South was not only ready to cut all connection with the North, but also to return to any political relation to England that England might be willing to form with it" [J.W. Cowell, *Southern Secession: A Letter Addressed to Captain M.T. Maury, Confederate Navy, &c,* London, 1862, p 65.]

[1862] The same writer, Cowell, expressed his own views to Captain Maury: "Virginia and Carolina will not belie [by compromising with the North] their English...descent. We...are your proper fellow-countrymen, and did we know you, or did you know us, we should mutually acknowledge each other as such." [*Ibid.*, p 19.] (There is much more in this vein in Cowell's writings.)

[1864] In December of 1864, when the Confederacy was clearly (except to Englishmen) failing, a Southern diarist wrote: "Some proposed to enter into Colonial or other subordinate relations with European nations. The Sentinel [often cited as the official C.S. Government organ] counselled the Confederate States to resume their places as the colonies of England, France, and Spain—like prodigal sons, or like young birds that had broken their shells too soon." [J.M. Callahan, *The Diplomatic History of the Southern Confederacy,* Baltimore, 1901, p 241.]

[c. 1867] An Englishman, who travelled in Virginia after the war, wrote: "Another gentleman I had met during the day had said to me, that 'he and many others wished they were living under a king of the English royal family. That Virginians deeply regretted that they had ever been separated from England; but that it was their own doing; for, if they had not helped, the Yankees never could have brought about the separation alone.'" The traveller adds that in Richmond "the people in bearing and conversation far more closely resemble Englishmen than is the case in the North. They speak, too, more frequently, and with more regard, of the old country, its people, and its institutions." [F.B. Zincke, *Last Winter in the United States,* London, 1868, pp 72 & 88.]

In addition to the foregoing references bearing on actual political union, there are almost innumerable pamphlet and other comments on the kinship between England and the South, the close but unspecified bonds that were to exist, and the community of interests already in existence.

Bibliography

A Note On Sources

The major studies of England in relation to the war for Southern independence are, curiously, all American: E.D. Adams, D. Jordan with E.J. Pratt, and F.L. Owsley. With regard to English opinion, especially pro-Southern opinion, Owsley, a Southerner, is the most useful and illuminating. There are valuable shorter studies, such as that by M. Beloff, and the varying treatments of the subject in the standard histories of the nineteenth century. There are also studies of special aspects or incidents of the war, such as those of R.H. Dana and T.L. Harris on the *Trent* crisis, and J.M. Callahan's diplomatic history of the Confederacy, and Captain J.D. Bulloch's most useful account of the Confederate secret service, of which in England he was himself the head. Finally, there are the biographies, not only of eminent Englishmen but of eminent Southerners, such as Commissioner Mason, and eminent Americans, such as Minister Adams.

The most obvious contemporary sources for English opinion are *Hansard* and *The Times,* to which so many other newspapers turned both for news and interpretive opinion. However, *The Times* (and other journals) has been examined with great thoroughness, beginning with Sir Leslie Stephen's indictment of it in 1865, continuing through E.D. Adams, particularly, and ending with its own history of itself. *Hansard* has also been thoroughly studied, although there is reason (see pp 97-98 above) to regard Parliament as a less reliable guide to the sympathies of England than one might expect it to be.

Less obvious, perhaps, and more valuable are various collections of letters that have become available, such as the Gladstone-Palmerston correspondence or the Disraeli papers. Also less obvious and still more valuable are the four volumes of Louis Blanc's contemporary reports to his native France on the state of England: his sympathies were Northern; his observation was sharp; he was, naturally but not inevitably, interested in opinion; and he is very readable. There is *no* source of contemporary opinion more valuable.

For this study, the primary source has been the pamphlet literature on the war between the American states. There is an immense number of these pamphlets—this bibliography is not exhaustive (except perhaps of the Bodleian Library's collection)—and most of them have apparently never been used before. In some cases they were, one supposes, printed at their author's own expense; and they are valuable, not only as a hitherto unexamined source of their attitudes and opinions but also and particularly because of their frankness and lack of restraint. The Englishman with something to say or to advocate, about which perhaps he felt passionately, and which might for reasons of policy be unacceptable to the journals, wrote a pamphlet. And, again, these pamphlets are the principal source for this work. The titles are themselves an interesting indication of opinion.

Bibliography
(P indicates Pamphlet, English unless marked 'American' or 'Southern')

A

Lord Acton, J.E.E. Dalberg-Acton, 1st Baron Acton,
   "American Diaries", *Fortnightly Review,* v 110-111, London, 1921.
   "The Civil War in America: Its Place in History" (originally a
      speech of 18 Jan. 1866 at Bridgnorth), *Historical Essays &*

Studies (ed., J.N. Figgis & R.V. Laurence), London, 1907. (very useful)

The History of Freedom & Other Essays, London, 1907.

Letters of Lord Acton to Mary, Daughter of the Right Hon. W.E. Gladstone (ed., Herbert Paul), London, 1904

C.F. Adams, Jr, *Charles Francis Adams,* London, 1900.

The Confederacy & the Transvaal, London, 1902. P-American *Studies Military & Diplomatic, 1775-1865,* New York, 1911. (with Henry Adams) *A Cycle of Adams Letters, 1861-1865* (ed., W.C. Ford), 2 vol., Boston, Mass. & New York, 1920.

Henry Adams, *The Education of Henry Adams,* London, 1919.

E.D. Adams, *Great Britain & the American Civil War,* 2 vol., London, 1925, (very useful)

W.E. Adams, *Our American Cousins,* London, 1883.

C.B. Adderly, MP, *Letter...on the Present Relations of England with the Colonies,* London, 1862. P

Ajax, *Social Wastes & Waste Lands: Flax v. Slave-Grown Cotton,* London, 1862. P

Americus, *Essay on the American War,* Liverpool, 1865. P

Anon.—

Anent the United States & Confederate States of North America, London, 1862. P

Anent the American War, London, 1865. P

Anent the North American Continent, London, 1864. P

Case of the Seizure of the Southern Envoys, London, 1861. P

The Civil War & Slavery in the United States, London, 1862. P—American

The Case of the Trent Examined, London, 1862. P

The Democratic Charter of the Future, &c., London, 1870. P

How Shall We Supply Our Cotton Market, London, 1862. P

A Plea for the South, London, [1864]. P

Public Policy, Personal Feeling & the Treaty of Washington, London, 1872. P

The Puppet Parliament of Earl Russell, K.G., London, 1866. P

Recognition of The Southern Confederacy, London, 1863. P

Refutation of Fallacious Arguments Anent the American Question, London, 1863. P

Russia, America, France, & England Passing through the Fire to Mars, Moloch, & Mammon, Edinburgh, 1863. P

Anon., ed., *American Thanksgiving Dinner,* London, 1863. P

Matthew Arnold, *Mixed Essays,* London, 1879.

R.A. Arnold, *The History of the Cotton Famine,* London, 1864.

Rev. William Arthur, *English Opinion of the American Rebellion,* Manchester, [1863]. P

Evelyn Ashley, MP, *Life of Henry John Temple, Viscount Palmerston, 1846-1865,* 2 vol., London, 1876

B

W.E. Baxter, MP, *The Social Condition of the Southern States of America,* London, 1862. P

Mrs A.P. Bayman, *Notes & Letters on the American War by an English "Lady",* London, 1864. P

B.D., *Federals & Confederates: For What Do They Fight? The True Issue of the American Civil War Stated,* London, 1862. P

H.W. Beecher, *American Rebellion,* (Report of Speeches of the Reverend Henry Ward Beecher Delivered at Public Meetings), Manchester, 1864.

M. Beloff, "Great Britain & the American Civil War", *History,* XXXVII (February 1952) 40-48. (very useful)

M. Bernard, Chichele Professor of International Law & Diplomacy, All Souls, Oxford, *Historical Account of the Neutrality of Great Britain During the American Civil War,* London, 1870.
A Lecture on Alleged Violations of Neutrality by England in the Present War, London, 1863. P
Two Lectures on the Present American War, Oxford, 1861. P

E.B. Bigelow, *The Tariff Question, &c.,* Boston, Mass., 1862. P-American.

John Bigelow, *Lest We Forget: Gladstone, Morley & the Cotton Loan of 1863,* New York, 1905

Louis Blanc, *Letters on England,* (transl.), 2 vol., London, 1866.
Letters on England, Second Series (transl.), 2 vol., London, 1867.

M.L. Bonham, Jr, *British Consuls in the Confederacy,* New York, 1911.

A.L. Bowey, *England's Foreign Trade in the 19th Century,* London, 1905.

J.B. Brebner, *North Atlantic Triangle,* New Haven, Conn., [1945].

A.C. Brice, *Indian Cotton Supply...for Relief to Lancashire,* Cornhill, 1863. P

British & Foreign Anti-Slavery Society, Tracts on America:—
  (1) *What the South is Fighting for?*, London, 1863. P
  (3) *British Aid to the Confederacy,* London, 1863. P
James Bryce, *The American Commonwealth,* 2 vol., London, 1893.
G.E. Buckle, *The Life of Benjamin Disraeli, Earl of Beaconsfield,*
  v IV: 1855-1868, London, 1916.
Captain J.D. Bulloch, C.S.N., *The Secret Service of the Confederate
  States in Europe,* 2 vol., London, 1883.

C

J.E. Cairns, *England's Neutrality in the American Contest,* London,
  1864. P
J.M. Callahan, *The Diplomatic History of the Southern
  Confederacy,* Baltimore, 1901.
Cambridge History of British Foreign Policy: see A.P. Newton.
Lord Campbell, *Speech of Lord Campbell in the House of Lords on
  the Right of the Neutral Powers to Acknowledge the Southern
  Confederacy,* London, 1863. P
Rev. G. Carlyle, Ed., *Proceedings of the Geneva Conference of the
  Evangelical Alliance, Held in September, 1861,* Edinburgh &
  London, 1862.
Captain C.C. Chesney, Professor of Military History at Sandhurst,
  A Military View of Recent Campaigns in Virginia & Maryland,
  2 vol, London, 1863. (very useful)
O.F. Christie, *The Transition from Aristocracy 1832-1867,* London,
  1927.
R.S.H. Church, *The Two Rebellions, &c.,* London, 1865.
  P—Southern(?)
W.S. Churchill, "If Lee Had Not Won at Gettysburg" in *If It Had
  Happened Otherwise* (Ed., J.C. Squire), London, 1931.
  The World Crisis 1911-1914, London, 1923.
Civis Anglicus, *A Voice from the Motherland Answering Mrs. H.
  Beecher Stowe's Appeal,* London, 1863. P
C. Clark, *The Trent & San Jacinto,* London, 1862. P
The Clergy of the Confederate States of America, *Address to
  Christians Throughout the World,* London, 1863. P—Southern
J.P. Cobbett, *Causes of the Civil War in the United States,* London,
  1861. P
M.D. Conway, *Autobiography,* 2 vol., London, 1904

J.W. Cowell, *France & the Confederate States,* London & Paris, 1865. P

Lancashire's Wrongs & the Remedy, London, 1863. P

Southern Secession: A Letter Addressed to Captain M.T. Maury, Confederate Navy on his Letter to Admiral Fitzroy, London, 1862. P

D

R.H. Dana, *The "Trent" Affair, An Aftermath,* Cambridge, Mass., 1912.

A.I. Dasent, *John Thadeus Delane, Editor of "The Times", His Life & Correspondence,* London, 1908.

Jefferson Davis, *The Rise & Fall of the Confederate Government,* 2 vol., London, 1881.

Canon de Haerne, Member of Belgian Chamber, *The American Question,* London, 1863. P

Alexis de Tocqueville, *Democracy in America,* (1st published 1835 & 1840), Oxford, [1946].

Benjamin Disraeli, *Lothair,* (1st published 1870), London, [1927].

W.H. Dixon, *The New America,* 2 vol., London, 1867.

J.W. Du Bose, *The Life & Times of William Lowndes Yancey,* Birmingham, 1892.

T.H. Dudley, U.S. Consul at Liverpool (during war), *Three Critical Periods in Our Diplomatic Relations with England during the Late War,* A reprint from *The Pennsylvania Magazine of History,* April, 1893.

W.A. Dunning, *The British Empire & The United States,* London, 1914.

E

F.M. Edge, *The Alabama & the Kearsarge,* 1864. P

The Destruction of the American Carrying Trade: A Letter to Earl Russell, K.G., London, 1863. P

England's Danger & her Safety, London, 1864. P

Great Britain & the United States, London, 1869. P

President's Lincoln's Successor, London, 1864. P

Stanley Elkins & Eric McKitrick, "A Meaning for Turner's Frontier: II The Southwest Frontier", *Political Science Quarterly,* LXIX (Dec. 1954) 4, pp 565-602, New York.

Erich Eyck, *Gladstone,* London, [1938].

F

Fair-Play, *The True State of the American Question, &c.,* London 1862. P—American.

W.F. Fergusson, *The Dearth of Cotton, &c.,* London, 1863. P

E.W. Field & C.G. Loring, *Correspondence on the Present Relations between Great Britain & the United States of America,* Boston, Mass, 1862. P

Captain Flack, *A Hunter's Experiences in the Southern States of America,* London, 1866.

C.R.L. Fletcher, *An Introductory History of England, 1815-1880,* New York, [1923].

G.F. Forbes, *Cultivation & Supply of Cotton in South America* [i.e., the Southern states], London, 1866.

W.C. Ford, ed.—see C.F. Adams, *A Cycle.*

D.S. Freeman, *R.E. Lee,* 4 vol., London & New York, 1935.

H. Fuller, *The Causes & Consequences of the Civil War in America,* London, [1862]. P—American

G

F.P. Gaines, *The Southern Plantation,* New York, 1924.

F.W. Gibbs, C.B., *The Foreign Enlistment Act,* London, 1863. P *Recognition: a Chapter from the History of the North American & South American States,* London, 1863. P

F.E. Gillespie, *Labour & Politics in England, 1850-1867,* Durham, N.C., 1931.

Paul Gottfried, "Through European Eyes", *The Southern Partisan,* Summer 1985.

T.C. Grattan, *England & the Disrupted States of America,* London, 1861. P

Mrs Rose Greenhow, *My Imprisonment & the First Year of Abolition Rule at Washington,* London, 1863. P—Southern

Anne Grimshaw, "Confederates Abroad: King Cotton & Loyal Lancashire", *The Southern Partisan,* Winter 1984.

Mrs H. Grote, *The Personal Life of George Grote,* London, 1873.

F.J. Grund, *Aristocracy in America,* 2 vol., London, 1839.

P. Guedalla, Ed., *Gladstone & Palmerston,* London, 1928. (Letters 1851-65)

H

H. Duncan Hall, *The British Commonwealth of Nations,* London, 1920

Newman Hall, *The American War, A Lecture to Working Men,* London, 1862. P

Hansard's Parliamentary Debates, Third Series, v CLXI to CLXXVIII.

T.L. Harris, *The Trent Affair,* Indianapolis, Indiana, [1896].

Sir John Hay, Bart., *The Reward of Loyalty,* Edinburgh, 1862.

A.J.B. Beresford Hope, *A Popular View of the American Civil War,* London, 1861. P (very useful)
  England, the North, & the South, London, 1862 (2nd edition). P
  The Social & Political Bearings of the American Disruption, London, 1863. P

John H. Hopkins, Bishop of Vermont [?], *The Bible View of American Slavery,* London, 1863. P—American

E.M. Hudson, *The Second War of Independence in America,* London, 1863.

James Hunt, PhD, President Anthropological Society of London, &c., *On the Negro's Place in Nature,* London, 1863. P

J

Evan John, *Atlantic Impact 1861,* London, [1952].

W.D. Jones, "The British Conservatives & the American Civil War" (a study of the Disraeli Papers), *The American Historical Review,* LVIII (April 1953)3, pp 527-543.

D. Jordan & E.J. Pratt, *Europe & the American Civil War,* Boston, Mass, 1931.

Col. T. Jordan, C.S.A., *The South: its Products, Commerce, & Resources,* London, 1861. P—Southern

K

J.H. Kennaway, M.A., *On Sherman's Track, or, The South After the War,* London, 1867.

L

A Lawyer, *The Coming Struggle in America,* Ayr, 1861. P

R.E. Leader, *Life & Letters of J.A. Roebuck,* London, 1897.

W.E.H. Lecky, *Democracy & Liberty,* 2 vol, London, 1899.

C. Lempriere, D.C.L., St. John's, Oxford, *The American Crisis Considered,* London, 1861.

L. Levi, *History of British Commerce, 1763-1878,* London, 1880.

W.S. Lindsay, Speech in the House of Commons 18 July 1862— See 'Nemo'.

C.G. Loring Correspondence—See E.W. Field.

Stephen Locke, *English Sympathies & Opinions Regarding the Late American Civil War,* London, 1866. (very useful) P

Lord Lothian, W.S.R. Kerr, Eighth Marquess of Lothian, *The Confederate Secession,* London & Edinburgh, 1864. (very useful)

L.S.—See Sir Leslie Stephen.

M

Helen MacDonald, *Canadian Public Opinion on the American Civil War,* N.Y., 1926.

F.W. Maitland, *Life & Letters of Leslie Stephen,* London, 1906.

T. Martin, *The Life of His Royal Highness, the Prince Consort,* 5 vol., London, 1880.

Karl Marx & F. Engels, *The Civil War in the United States,* London, [1938]. (Originally articles in New York & Vienna papers 1861-62, & correspondence 1861-66, collected & edited by Richard Emmale.)

Virginia Mason, *The Public Life & Diplomatic Correspondence of James A. Mason,* New York, 1906.

Rev. J.W. Massie, *The American Crisis in Relation to the Anti-Slavery Cause,* London, 1862. P
America: the Origin of Her Present Conflict: Her Prospect for the Slave, & Her Claim for Anti-Slavery Sympathy, London, 1864. P

R.L. Maury, *A Brief Sketch of the Work of Matthew Fontaine Maury During the War, 1861-1865,* Richmond-in-Virginia, 1915. P—Southern

Capt. F.A. Maxse, R.N., *Pro Patria...,* London, 1863.

Justin McCarthy, *A History of Our Own Times,* 4 vol., London, 1880. (very useful)

M.J. McHaffie, *Was it a Cotton Famine?,* London, 1865. P

G. McHenry, *The Cotton Trade: its Bearing upon the Prosperity of Great Britain and Commerce of the American Republics Considered in Connection with the System of Negro Slavery in the Confederate States,* London, 1863.

James M. McPherson, *Battle Cry of Freedom: The Era of the Civil War,* New York, 1988.

R.D. Meade, *Judah P. Benjamin, Confederate Statesman,* New York, 1943.

G. M'Henry, *The Cotton Supply of the United States of America,* London, 1865. P—American

J.S. Mill, "The Contest in America", *Fraser's Magazine,* Feb., 1862.
Lord Robert Montagu, *A Mirror in America,* London, 1861.
C.S. Morehead, *Southern Confederation,* Liverpool, 1862.
S.E. Morison & H.S. Commager, *The Growth of the American
    Republic,* 2 vol., New York, 1942.
J. Morley, *The Life of William Ewart Gladstone,* 3 vol., London 1903.
R.B. Mowat, *The Diplomatic Relations of Great Britain & the
    United States,* London, 1925.
Eugene Musson, *Letter to Napoleon III on Slavery in the Southern
    States,* London, 1862. P—American

N

Nemmo, *Earl Russell, K.G., & the Foreign Office,* London, 1864. P
Nemo, *Remarks on the Policy of Recognizing the Independence of the
    Southern States of North America,* London, 1863. (Appendix con-
        tains W.S. Lindsay's speech in Parliament of 18 July 1862.) P
J.A. Nevins, Ed., *America Through British Eyes,* New York, 1948.
F.W. Newman, *Character of the Southern States of America,*
    Manchester, 1863.
A.P. Newton, "Anglo-American Relations during the Civil War",
    in the *Cambridge History of British Foreign Policy,* v II,
        1815-1866, Camb., 1923.
H.G. Nicholas, *"Uncle Tom's Cabin 1852-1952",* History Today,
    II(June 1952)6.
John Noble, Jr, *Arbitration & a Congress of Nations as a Substitute
    for War,* London, 1862. P
Non-Elector, *The Approaching Dissoution: or Support the
    Government,* London, 1865. P
Non-Elector—Conservative, *The Claims of Conservatism v.
    Liberal Liberality,* London, 1865. (Answer to preceding). P
Anne Norton, *Alternative Americas: A Reading of Antebellum Political
    Culture,* Chicago, 1986.

O

L. Oliphant, M.P., *On the Present State of Political Parties in
    America,* London, 1866. P
Onesimus Secundus, *The True Interpretation of the American
    Civil War & of England's Cotton Difficulty, &c.,* London, 1863. P
R.G. Osterweis, *Romanticism & Nationalism in the Old South,* New
    Haven, Connecticut, 1949.

F.L. Owsley, *King Cotton Diplomacy,* Chicago, [1931]. (very useful)
Rev. T.D. Ozanne, *The South as It Is,* London, 1863.

P

J.A. Partridge, Reform Club, *The False Nation or Why the South
    Can't Stand,* London, 1864. P
Henry Pelling, *America & the British Left,* London, [1956].
Philo-Americanus, *The American Struggle. An Appeal to the
    People of the North,* London, 1862. P
F.S. Pulling, *The Life & Speeches of the Marquis of Salisbury, K.G.,*
    2 vol., London, 1885.

R

A Recent Tourist, *The Right of Recognition, a Sketch of the Present
    Policy of the Confederate States,* London, 1862. P
W.B. Reed, *A Northern Plea for Peace,* London, 1863.
    P—American
S.J. Reid, *Lord John Russell,* London, 1895.
J.F. Rhodes, *Lectures on the American Civil War Delivered Before
    the University of Oxford in...1912,* New York, 1913.
    *History of the United States from the Compromise of 1850 to the
    McKinley-Bryan Campaign of 1896,* 8 vol., New York, 1920.
J.D. Richardson, *Messages & Papers of the Confederacy,* Nashville,
    1906.
E.Y. Robbins, *An Impartial View of the War in America, &c.,*
    London, 1864. ('Impartially' considered, the South are traitorous
    dogs.) P—American
J.A. Roebuck, *The Colonies of England,* London, 1849.
Alfred Rooker, *Does it Answer? Slavery in America, a History,*
    London, 1864. P
Earl Russell, *Recollections & Suggestions, 1813-1873,* London, 1875.
W.H. Russell, Correspondent of *The Times,* (in America until 1861),
    Civil War in America, Boston, Mass., 1861.
    My Diary North & South, 2 vol., London, 1863.

S

Lord Saint Leonard, *The Case of the Alexandra,* London, 1864. P
F.W. Sargent, *England, the United States, & the Southern
    Confederacy,* London, 1864. P—American
L.M. Sears, *John Slidell,* Durham, N.C., 1925.

F. Seebohm, *The Crisis of Emancipation in America,* London, 1865.
Sir John R. Seeley, *Expansion of England,* London, 1883.
Jonathan Slingsby (Pseud.), *A Familiar Epistle to Robert J. Walker,
    &c.,* London, 1863. P—American
Goldwin Smith, *Does the Bible Sanction Slavery?,* Oxford &
    London, 1863. P
    England & America, a Lecture, Manchester, 1865. P
    Letter to a Whig Member of the S.I.A. [Southern Independence
        Association], London, 1864. P
Samuel Smith, *The Cotton Trade of India,* London, 1863. P
P.A. Smith, *The Seizure of the Southern Commissioners, &c.,*
    London, 1862. P
D.C. Somervell, *English Thought in the Nineteenth Century,* N.Y.,
    1929.
A Southern Lady, *The Woes of War: A Letter of Sorrow* (Preface
    by an English lady, Pauline Vyver), London, 1862. P—Southern
James Spence, *The American Union,* Its Effect on National Character
    & Policy, &c., London, 1862. (Probably most widely read book
        of war.) (very useful)
    On the Recognition of the Southern Confederacy, London, 1862. P
    Southern Independence: an Address, &c., London & Glascow,
        1863. P
J.H. Stack, *Historic Doubts Relative to the American War,*
    Birmingham, 1862. P
Lady Augusta Stanley, *Letters of a Young Lady at Court 1849-1863,*
    London, 1927.
*Sir Leslie Stephen ['L.S.'], The "Times" on the American War:
    A Historical Study,* London, 1865. P
W.W. Story, *The American Question,* London, 1862.

T
C. Taylor, *The Probable Causes & Consequences of the American
    War,* Liverpool & London, 1864. (An English answer to:—) P
W. Taylor, *Cause & Probable Results of the Civil War in America:
    Facts for the People of Great Britain,* London, 1862.
        P—American
W.M. Thackeray, *Esmond,* London, 1852.
    The Virginians, 2 vol., London, 1859. (Published serially
        1858-1859)

Frank Thistlethwaite, "America & the Two Nations of Englishmen", *The Virginia Quarterly Review,* XXXI (Autumn 1955)4, pp 505-525.
Margaret Thorp, *Female Persuasion: Six Strong-Minded Women,* New Haven, Conn., 1949.
The Times, *The History of the Times: The Tradition Established 1841-1884,* (v II) London, 1939.
Rev. F.W. Tremlett, *Christian Brotherhood: Its Claims & Duties; with a Special Reference to... War in America,* London, [1864].
G.M. Trevelyan, *British History in the Nineteenth Century and After (1782-1919),* London, 2nd edition, 1937.
English Social History, London, [1944].
A.J. Toynbee, *A Study of History:* vol. IV, London, 1939.
Robert Trimble, *The Negro, North & South: the Status of the Coloured Population in the Northern & Southern States of America Compared,* London, 1863. P
Review of the American Struggle, London, 1864. P
Slavery in the United States of North America, London, 1863. P

V

B. Villiers & W.H. Chesson, *Anglo-American Relations, 1861-1865,* London, [1919].
C.A. Vince, *John Bright, M.A.,* London, 1898.

W

R.J. Walker, *American Finances & Resources,* London, 1863.
Jefferson Davis & Repudiation, London, 1863. P—American
S. Walpole, *A History of England from the Conclusion of the Great War in 1815,* 5 vol., London, 1878.
The Life of Lord John Russell, 2 vol., London, 1889.
J. Watts, PhD, *The Facts of the Cotton Famine,* Manchester, 1866.
T. Weed & Others, *The Life of Thurlow Weed,* 2 vol., Boston, Mass., 1883-84.
J. Westlake, Barrister, &c., *Commercial Blockades,* London, 1862. P
White Republican, *The Flag of Truce,* London, 1862. P—American
A.D. White, *A Letter to William Howard Russell, LL.D., on Passages in His 'Diary North & South',* London, 1863. P
James Williams, *Rise & Fall of the Model Republic,* London, 1863. P
The South Vindicated, London, 1862. P

W.E. Williams, *The Rise of Gladstone to the Leadership of the
    Liberal Party 1859-1868,* Cambridge, 1934.
E.L. Woodward, *The Age of Reform 1815-1870,* Oxford, [1949].

XYZ

Edward Yates, *A Letter to the Women of England on Slavery in the
    Southern States of America: Considered Especially in Reference
    to the Condition of the Female Slaves, &c.,* London, 1863. P
G.M. Young, *Early Victorian England 1830-1865,* 2 vol., London,
    [1934].
F.B. Zincke, *Last Winter in the United States,* London, 1868.